Wounded to Win

Finding Purpose in Pain

Njiba Tirado

Foreword by Leia Hardimon

To

Dr. David Lemba-Lemba Kasonga & Maman Nadine

Muadi-Mayonga Tshibangu,

Out of your union in marriage, I was birthed.

I wish I had more time on earth with you.

May your existence live forever in my heart and through the stories written in this book.

I love you.

TABLE OF CONTENTS

FOREWORD

"She's gone. Leia… she's gone."

The words hit me like bricks, but also floated over me like they were for someone else. My mind raced, who is gone? He can't mean Traci. I pulled my car over to figure out what to say, what to ask and to listen. I hear crying, I hear, "She was so sick…," "You were such a good friend," "yesterday," "She made me promise not to tell you." I don't remember much more of our conversation. I sat sobbing in a church parking lot for a few minutes and then began to drive home. When I got home, I remember telling John that she's gone and then collapsing on the bed in tears. He, as shocked as I was, asked questions, none of which I had any answers to. Somehow, Trinity got to school, and I moved to a chair in my living room, where I'm pretty sure I spent the next three days.

This was by far the most immense pain I'd ever experienced. It sucked the breath out of me; it created spirals of confusion, anger and sorrow that consumed my mind. I stared out the window feeling lost. I heard John, in the background, calling to cancel commitments I had for that day, arranging rides for the kids, making sure I had food and I'm sure trying to find things to comfort me. I don't remember much of this other than knowing it was being taken care of. That is love… I am so grateful for the love of a spouse that just picked up the pieces and carried me until I could function.

After a few days, I came to the realization that my kids and family needed me to participate in life and that Tito needed my help to arrange for a funeral here in Dallas. Having a purpose and a task, a mission to honor her gave me some strength. For a month or two tears were constantly three seconds from rolling down my face. My emotions were so raw and exposed. I would robot through my required appearances in public and then go sleep all the hours I could. John pressed in—asking all the questions about how I was coping with it, what I was feeling, bringing me small gifts to affirm that he was there. He tried—he really did. I was just good at hiding how deep my pain was. I planned her funeral here in Dallas. I chose a beautiful plot next to her son and planned for her to be placed there in a month or so when Tito was able to make the trip to Dallas. I chose not to fly to Virginia for the memorial because we had this other service planned. Our family and friends that were part of our lives with the Tirados were all here and it made sense to mourn her loss with them.

An unfortunate miscommunication between Pastor Tito and I occurred. He decided not to have the service in Dallas. I felt that I had been robbed of the opportunity to love her through her illness, robbed of the goodbye I should have been there for and now I was robbed of even being able to pay respects to her. There was no closure, no resolve, and it only fueled the cloud of depression and anger that I was sinking into.

I tried to process my emotions because that is what we are told to do. Let me be clear, I did not want to process anything. I was angry. Angry at Pastor Tito, I was angry at Traci for lying to me, for hiding the full truth, for making me think things were better, for not trusting me with the biggest secret of her whole life. I was angry at myself. I should have known, I should have gone to her birthday, I should I have picked up on the cues; how could I be her best friend and not be there at the end? Angry at God. Why did He take her? Doesn't He know she has a child that needs her FOREVER?! Did He forget that we prayed hours for her healing? Did He care? I even got mad at John. How could he have not known and made Tito tell me!?

I was sad. There is a deeper type of sadness that comes with feeling betrayed. The betrayal that she didn't love me enough to tell me the truth was paralyzing. My perspective was selfish, but no matter how I asked God the questions, the answers I wanted were selfish. I was hurt. I shut everyone out. I literally said the words "I don't want to ever have friends again because losing them hurts too much." Relationally I pushed everyone away, including my best Dallas friends. I acted as though everything was fine, but I put very big boundaries on how close anyone could get. Pushing back wasn't only my response to friends, but also to God. I stopped talking to Him about anything personal. My prayer life went to 50%. I never stopped believing the truth of the Bible or the importance of all the disciplines of the faith—I just didn't trust Him with anything that could hurt my heart again.

I poured myself into my family, the preschool ministry I was starting, my dance studio, and I buried my feelings in work. I created so much work and business that I barely had time to think. I would homeschool the girls, drive them everywhere, work my preschool ministry job, teach 4–5 hours of dance, feed everyone, and then get on the computer and handle the marketing for both my dance studio and the new MOPS ministry I was working on. I was sleeping 4–6 hours a night and not even that was restful. If you ever take a lifeguarding class they will tell you that drowning doesn't mean flailing arms and calling for help. It's most often silent and with little movement. That was how I mourned: silent and moving only as much as required to function in the business I had created. Inside, I was screaming HELP! I was flailing my arms in fear of losing anyone I loved.

Grief comes in waves and the waves come less frequently as time passes. Then, all of a sudden, BOOM—you are hit by what seems like a tsunami of grief and it knocks the breath out of you, and you feel like you're right back in the car hearing the words "she's gone" again. Numbness becomes a way of functioning through work, kids, obligations, commitments, but you can't listen to many sermons and be okay sitting in that numbness. Gradually, after a few of "those" Sunday services (the ones where you know you need to do something, but you don't do it yet) I recognized I couldn't live in that numbness, so I bought a few books on grief and gave a very weak attempt at healing.

One day, my daughter Trinity was going through some rough things at school, and she said the words, "I don't want to have friends because it hurts too much when they leave you." Her words hit me like a ton of bricks. Those were my words! I had said that many times when people tried to connect with me or when invited to do things. It had been my motto and now, now it was my daughter's burden. It immediately became clear that the pain I was dealing with was being transferred to my kids and the choices I was making about how to deal with that pain were becoming the choices that my girls were making. I realized in an instant that every relationship my kids had from that day forward was being affected by my grief and my pain. Without having any reason, they were taking the walls I'd put up and extending them over their hearts. Something broke in me. Shortly after, there was a song that my iTunes selected for me one day and something about it connected with where I was. I clung to that song and played it on repeat for two months. I told myself to sing the words until I believed them.

GUNGOR - beautiful things

All this pain

I wonder if I'll ever find my way

I wonder if my life could really change at all

All this earth

Could all that is lost ever be found

Could a garden come up from this ground at all

You make beautiful things

You make beautiful things out of the dust

You make beautiful things

You make beautiful things out of us

All around

Hope is springing up from this old ground

Out of chaos life is being found in You

You make beautiful things

You make beautiful things out of the dust

You make beautiful things

You make beautiful things out of us

You make beautiful things

You make beautiful things out of the dust

You make beautiful things

You make beautiful things out of us

You make me new, You are making me new

You make me new, You are making me new

You make beautiful things

You make beautiful things out of the dust

You make beautiful things

You make beautiful things out of us

Gradually God delivered exactly what I was making my mouth proclaim with each repeat, but it took time… is taking time.

During my period of being completely lost and depressed… life was moving on for Tito. John and Tito talked numerous times in the months following the loss of Traci. He had grieved her for so long—even while she was living, and God was working different things out in him. John softly broke the news to me when Tito began seeing Njiba and despite my screaming and crying fits about it being wrong for him to be with anyone ever… he patiently talked to me and explained the heart of Tito and what God seemed to be doing. I was away at a retreat when my husband called and said, "I don't want you to see it on Facebook and get upset… Tito got married." I quietly got up from my chair and went to my bedroom. I cried and cried. This moment made it so final, so real, so permanent. I guess somewhere in my mind it seemed she would just come back. I know it's ridiculous, but if he's married, she really must be gone!

A bit later in the year I was preparing Christmas gift lists and had a few items that I wanted to send Christian. I had been praying for him, for his heart and for his memories of his mom to remain strong but felt awkward about talking to him. For some reason as I was making that list the conversation I had with Traci when she said the actual words, "You have to love whoever Tito marries" flashed through my mind. The kind of memory where you remember exactly where you were, what you were wearing, what you were holding. The kind of memory we use when describing 9-11 or some huge moment of impact. Instantly it became clear I had to reach out to Njiba and at least try to form a civil relationship with her. I mean how weird is this call? "Hi—I'm your husband's widow's best friend… and ummm I'm supposed to love you."

I chose to send a Facebook message to her and just ask if I could mail the gifts to him and congratulated her on the marriage. She responded so graciously and so lovingly to me that I felt all the walls I had built up in my heart about her crack. Within an instant I felt the strangest connection with a stranger I've ever had. The only explanation is the Holy Spirit united our hearts. God intervened and put a connection together that normally would take years to build. She began sharing her heart for Christian and all the things he was doing. She even talked about Traci and her desire to keep her memory alive for Christian and wanting to honor her in their home. AND THEN SHE SAID THE CRAZIEST THING… she said that Traci's and my picture was still up in the house, and she talked to Christian often about us. Njiba talked about her compassion for my loss and grief and how difficult it must have been. We exchanged several messages and she said she had hoped to meet me and was so glad I reached out.

About three months later I got a message from Njiba sayings, "We would like to come to Dallas; can we maybe stay with you?" I have to admit I agreed mostly out of curiosity, obligation, love for Tito and Christian with major apprehension and fear. Satan would put thoughts in my head and try to make me angry and full of dislike and hate, but I kept repeating the song… "You make beautiful things out of dust… out of us." The moment she stepped in my home all the fear, worry, apprehension and rote obligation melted away. I felt the genuine love she had for Christian immediately. I could see the way she talked to him and the way she worked with him that she not only loved him, but God had knit in her heart the skills to be equipped to parent him. I saw his love and respect for her. God had given Christian a mom. My very worry that I'd screamed at Traci and God had been taken care of. I was supposed to love her because she's Christian's mom.

There are things in our lives that happen that we can't explain. Things that are not rational but are so very real. The Holy Spirit moves and breathes over us mending our hearts in ways that we cannot even imagine. My simple hope would have been that I would be allowed access to Christian and that Njiba would tolerate my presence in his life in a limited way. Instead, God knit the common love for Pastor Tito, Christian, dad, and Sam into a solid godly friendship that inspires us both. I'm supposed to love her **because there's no way I could know her and not.**

With Love,

Leia Hardimon

P.A.I.N

If you have ever bumped your small toe on anything, you are acutely aware that pain inflicted on even what seems to be the smallest part of your body can affect you drastically. As someone who has had a series of injuries from riding my bike, running when I shouldn't have been or playing sports, I know too well how pain to one part of my body causes my entire body not to be in equilibrium. Yet when I think of my multiple physical injuries, I chuckle. Why is that? One simple truth: I have the memories of the incidents, but not the pain attached to them.

What is pain? Though I could easily use the dictionary and give the academic definition of pain, I refused to look up what pain means. Pain and I have known each other long enough that I didn't believe defining it academically would be an adequate reflection of our long-standing friendship. So as the word brewed in my spirit and I pondered about this book, I laid in bed one morning and thought, what is pain? As quickly as I had interrogated myself, a still small voice within me responded, P.A.I.N. is ***Past or Present Actions Impacting Now.***

In one of his many sermons, my husband, Dr. Tito Tirado stated that "We do ourselves a disservice when we try to quantify pain." To be frank, pain is difficult to quantify because we all experience it differently. Losing a pet could seem very painful to a person who has never lost a human loved one. But someone who may have lost a family member to a gun shooting may deem the pain of losing a dog low on the pain scale. Kind of like when you go to the doctor and they say, "On a scale of 1 to 10, how bad is your pain?" While the quantity of physical and emotional pain is arguable, the truth of the matter is that many of us are no stranger to pain despite how it enters our life. There are different kinds of pain. Nevertheless, "Pain, stress, pressure, and anxiety are no respecter of culture. Pain doesn't discriminate. Pain does not care if you are black, white, Hispanic, male, female, married, single, divorced, the boss, the employee, a pastor, or a recent convert. Pain comes to us all" (Dr. Tito Tirado). Consequently, it is imperative that we as people aim to continuously find P.U.R.P.O.S.E. in our pain and process it through a riverbank that ultimately glorifies God.

While some pain like a paper cut or stepping on Legos can be short-lived, there are other pains, such as death, betrayal or abuse that pierce your soul beyond what seems imaginable. You know the pain that causes you to scream at the top of your lungs, God where are you? The type of pain that pushes you to suicidal thoughts or simply keeps you awake at night, while walking like a zombie by day. A pain that you can easily become numb to and smile your way through life, when in reality you are incarcerated but have yet to identify yourself with an inmate number. Yes, that kind of pain. I don't know what you thought of as you read these lines, but whatever it is you filled your pain blank with, I want to encourage you to join me on this journey of walking in wholeness and living victoriously.

REFLECTION

As your read those lines describing pain, what area(s) in your life present or past have caused you pain?

____

____

____

CHAPTER 1: OUR FIRST ENCOUTERS

Twenty-Three

Twenty-three is an odd number because it cannot be equally divided by two. Twenty-three is also a prime number because it only has two factors, one and itself. The dictionary defines odd as "different from what is usual or expected; strange." Prime, however is defined as "of first importance, main or of the best possible quality; excellent." No wonder ribs of excellence are called prime ribs. I am not sure that's how they got their name. Nonetheless, twenty-three is a significant number in my life. Though I enjoy watching basketball, twenty-three is not a reminder of Michael Jordan, LeBron James, or any other athlete's jersey. In addition, twenty-three does not represent any magical thing that happened to me. It is not my favorite number or the number of states in the United States I have visited. Twenty-three is not even how many members there are in my family nor is it my age. Twenty-three is simply an odd number that is also prime and happens to be the age gap between my husband and me. Now, while your mind may be racing to find out how old I am, let me assure you that I am a legal adult. Neither he nor I have committed anything illegal, immoral, unbiblical, or sinful. What we have committed however, is odd and prime. Though odd in the eyes of men, it is rather prime in the eyes of God. Our union cannot be equally divided into two groups because we have become one flesh through marriage. It is therefore also prime because it only has two factors, God, and itself. My name is Njiba Tirado. I am married to a pastor. I am a mom to a twenty-seven-year-old, thirteen-year-old and a one-year-old. I am a grandmother also known as Gigi to two grandchildren, who are three and two. I am an educator professionally whose teaching career started in room twenty-three with twenty-three students. Yet my journey to existence began far from Newport News, Virginia. The manifestation of the union between my parents, me, started in a country known as Cote-D'Ivoire.

Ivory Coast to the Democratic Republic of Congo

James 1 verse 2 urges the reader to "count it all joy when you fall into various trials," (NKJV) and continues with encouragement about the profits gained from trials. I would like to lie and say I have always found joy through my trials, but the reality is, I would be deceiving myself and you if I veered off from the emotional truth that falling into various trials left me wondering for many years if there was such a thing as joy. You see, in the beginning God created the heavens and the earth, and as my son Christian used to say, "and the people too." Somehow, He saw it fitting to land me in the continent of Africa, in Ivory Coast, on April 9th, 1991. I was birthed by a wonderful woman, whom I didn't know to appreciate until later in life and a man who worked extremely hard to provide for my well-being. It must have taken some months before I realized these two strangers were what we call mom and dad, or as we say in French, maman and papa. Along with them came a light skinned female who was four years older than me. I was told she was my big sister. Suzanne is her name. Yet culturally speaking, it would be impolite for me to address her by name without adding "yaya" in front of it as a sign of sisterhood hierarchy.

While I have little recollection of the years spent in Ivory Coast with these people, through pictures and stories, I gathered that we lived a decent life. My father was finishing his residency as an ophthalmologist, and mom fulfilled the duties of motherhood. There are photographs of us at parks, museums, parties, and home. One united, happy, and loving family. This is the world any child should know and cherish forever. But how does forever exist in such a fallen world, where our bodies eventually decay, and our spirit vanishes? Better yet, the unavoidable truth of life occurs, pain.

My first encounter with pain was in 1994 on our trip from Ivory Coast to the Democratic Republic of Congo, formally known as Zaire. My father had accepted a job in a small town named Tshikaji (chee-ka-jee). Tshikaji is located about ten miles outside of Kananga, the capital of the Kasai-Occidental Province. The hospital my father would be working at was called Good Shepherd Hospital, which gained its foundation in 1965. The hospital was started in partnership with the Presbyterian Church in the United States (PCUSA), an abbreviation I knew so little of until my arrival in the United States in 2002. Nevertheless, I can hardly remember much of our relocation trip, except the plane ride. After landing, I had to use the restroom. My mom told me to hurry as we were getting off the plane soon. Excited to simply be in the airplane, I went and handled my business like a big girl. After flushing the toilet, my biggest nightmare began. In my underdeveloped brain, I became incapable of opening a simple door. Having been on many planes now, I often laugh at this encounter. How could I be so stupid? I remember standing in the bathroom terrified at the thought of never seeing my parents again, or the plane taking off and my family forgetting my existence. Tears slowly rolled down my eyes as I banged on the door frantically. I can't recall knowing whether God existed or not, but I remember needing a savior at that exact moment. Little did I know, my mother on the other side was mortified at the thought that I wasn't by her side. I guess she thought I had been in there too long. After what felt like decades, a flight attendant came to my rescue and reunited me to my mother. I can vividly see her youthful, worried face as my small legs made their way to her. I hugged her tightly and she whispered, "Don't ever do that again." Wait a second! Did she think I was just building a sandcastle in the bathroom, hoping to be taken to the next destination? Was I truly capable of formulating such a ridiculous and outrageous idea? Well, according to those who knew me, anything was possible with Njiba. Yes, Njiba, formally known as Njiba Kasonga. I am the daughter of Dr. David and Mrs. Nadine Kasonga. I have an older sister named Suzanne. These people constituted the entirety of my existence up until that plane ride and for the very first time, pain demonstrated to me that my united, happy, loving family could be nonexistent.

Assimilating

The human brain is fascinating. There are some memories that we easily remember, while others go unnoticed for the long hall. It's difficult to say I recall adjusting to an unfamiliar environment. All I know is we lived in a decent home near the hospital where dad worked. We were surrounded by other medical employees in the neighborhood. We were fortunate enough to have all the necessities and even maids! I never knew how much of a luxury this was until I became an adult in America. If only I could rewind the time to not having to lift a finger. From what I remember, we lived the good life. My father was familiar with the town of Kananga and had many relatives there. Although his father passed away at the age of 56, his wife, my paternal grandmother, was still alive. With four of her sons living nearby, Kaku Mutanga as we called her, had her basic needs met. In addition, it was a tradition for the family to gather at her house on Sunday afternoons after church. Through these gathering, her sons bonded while the children spent time singing and playing games. In addition, we compared our lives to each other and aimed to prove which nuclear family was better, which was an ingredient for what I later discovered is called dysfunctional family relationships.

Nonetheless, there was a major contrast between my mom's side of the family and my dad's. While my dad's siblings had managed to become doctors, lawyers, nurses, ambassadors, missionaries, and professors, I knew nothing about what my maternal aunts and uncles did for a living. They mostly lived in a small village named Muene Ditu. My maternal grandfather, Kaku Celestin, worked in the market and grandma, Kaku Isa, seemed to always be home. I knew I had an uncle in Europe and an uncle in Kinshasa who was a lawyer. The rest of the family seemed to survive somehow. Yet despite the lack of prestigious social status, the love amid that family was beyond unnoticeable. My maternal aunts and uncles were attentive, gentle, and compassionate. We spent many vacations with them. Though they couldn't offer us much materialistically, their love was worth every second with them.

Everyone tells you how much of an influence your parents have on your life. No one ever speaks of the impact extended family has on one's life. Whether good or bad, their existence has a way of shaping our memories, which in turn shape us. It takes a village to raise a child, says the African proverbs. Yet the act of raising children demands an unconditional commitment to nurture despite nature. But sometimes nature ends up doing the nurturing and for me that often seemed to be the case. Because I cannot recollect all that Ivory Coast had to offer, my experiences are jumbled between the Democratic Republic of Congo and the United States. I would love to say that my memory is sharp, and I can trace the linear data of each point of my existence. But I can't. However, the memorable moments can be considered the outliers as they stick out unlike the rest.

In contrast to the public school system in the U.S., schools in the D.R. Congo had yearly fees. We wore uniforms. Everyone brought their lunch, if they could afford to. You were disciplined through corporal punishment when you misbehaved. There were no playgrounds or cafeterias. When you think of my elementary school, imagine two long one-story buildings parallel of each other. Each building was divided into classrooms from 1st grade through 6th grade. There were no windows or lights. The brick walls had rectangular openings that allowed the sun in. The floors were cemented, and the desks were made out of wood. The yard was mostly sand and required to be swept every Saturday. To the right of both buildings was a building for kindergarteners and the principal's office. To the left of both buildings were the bathrooms. Not the ones you're picturing in your head, toilet bowl, running water and the ability to flush. Nope! These bathrooms had stalls with a hole dug in the ground. No water to flush and no sink to wash your hands. Thinking about it, many Americans would not partake in using those bathrooms. *But when you don't have any other option, you choose what has been chosen for you.* Interesting enough, I remember experiencing great joy at my school, Mamu Lumingu. Our uniforms were white and blue. We went to school Monday through Saturday. Saturdays were half days because we spent them cleaning the entire school. With no janitors or custodians to clean after you, you become very aware of your responsibility for the upkeep of the property you use. As an educator who has worked in the school system in America, we could use a certain aspect of this methodology in our schools.

My earliest memory in elementary school occurs around the age of 3 or 4. I attended preschool near our home but seemed more advanced for it. This prompted my parents to have me tested for kindergarten. I passed the exams and began the journey of always being the youngest person in my classes. Though it seemed quite cool to be young and intelligent, there is no denying that being bullied disregarded that factor. I remember standing outside the door of my kindergarten class crying as my classmates laughed at me because I had just peed on myself. Why didn't I just ask for the bathroom? What could I have been doing that left me so distracted? Wasn't I potty-trained? Or did my habits of peeing in the bed at night shift to daylight? All questions I will never be able to answer. All I know is humiliation had already happened. I stood there for all the world to see, crying, and waiting for a new pair of clothes, wishing I could disappear. Or be the superhero with powers to be invisible and slap every kid who laughed at me. But unfortunately, all I could do was experience a different relationship with pain. Except this time, it was clothed as humiliation. By the age of 4, it was apparent that pain and I would be developing a long-lasting friendship. I always thought friendship equated happiness and joy. The older I became, the more I realized however, that friendships entail having a relationship, and sometime relationships are toxic.

Not to toot my own horn, but I was a smart girl academically. I started 1st grade by the age of 4 going on 5. I remember my pre-school and kindergarten teachers telling my parents I was too advanced for their class. Hearing these words boosted my ego at a young age and propelled the desire within me to always excel. Can you see the perfectionist problems later? Needless to say, I enjoyed going to school. One, I knew I was smart. Two, my parents were well off compared to others, so I had bragging rights. Three, I was a jerk. You mean there is a place where I can go for hours on end and perfect my craft of extreme sarcasm and smart mouthing? Sign me up.

In the Congo, the best schools were developed by Catholics. They were operated by priests and nuns. Every morning we recited prayers to the Virgin Mary and had religion class. Though I grew up protestant, going through the routine prayers and symbolisms became the norm. Despite the Catholicism, I thoroughly appreciated my time at Mamu Lumingu. My friendship with pain grew there in many ways. One, I recall attempting to fight multiple people. Two, my butt got spanked quite often for coming to school late. Three, I often allowed my mouth to get the best of me. I can remember my mother's face on multiple occasions after school gazing at me as she silently prayed, "Lord, what am I going to do with this child?" The reason I know it was so, is because as a mom now, I find myself staring at my children praying the same prayer.

The itching tree incident is a classic memory which allowed me to witness my mother's silent prayer face. When we moved to Tshikaji, we had a big open space at the front of the house. There were a few trees but not much scenery. My mom, like God walking in the Garden of Eden with Adam and Eve, told my sister and I that we couldn't touch a specific tree. If you don't know the story about Eve in the Bible, well, I'd rather not spoil the story. One afternoon, my buddy Yannick and I decided the forbidden tree was no longer forbidden. Yannick and his family lived across the street from us. His father was also a doctor who worked at the hospital with my father. Yannick and I became best buds. Oh, how I miss the age of innocence where boys and girls can be friends without any other thought crossing the brain. Nonetheless, on a sunny afternoon, with the wind blowing on our faces, Yannick and I took some small rocks, threw them at the forbidden tree and watched in suspense to see if anything magical would happen. The tree was tall and mostly green. It had small fruits that resembled grapes. As the rocks hit the fruits, a few of them fell on the ground. To satisfy our curiosity, we picked them up and squeezed them. Somehow, we knew they weren't meant to be eaten. However, squeezing them caused some clear liquid to ooze out of them. Ignorantly, we played with the juice and managed to apply it to our bodies. We stood there wondering what was so evil about this tree. It didn't take long for Yannick and me to discover that those small fruits, "matshatsha" cause skin irritation, along with strong, violent itching. We immediately started crying and ran to my mom in fear. As she opened the front door, she saw two children scratching themselves like monkeys. She sighed. She then made the silent prayer face. That afternoon, Yannick and I were forced to sit outside naked, covered with white flour to help with the itch. We were a public display of our shame. I wonder as a mother if that would be my punishment approach. But if God kicked Adam and Eve out of the garden, I suppose our humiliation wasn't bad after all. That day, I saw a glimpse of the consequences of disobedience. As I stood there naked and ashamed, it dawned on me that here was pain befriending me again. Only this time it was clothed in disobedience.

CHAPTER 2: IT WAS ALL A DREAM

Rainbow Babies

My husband and I got married on April 1st, 2016. Neither one of us thought it would be a great April fool's joke. However, we love watching people's faces when we tell them our wedding date. We are usually braced for questionable looks, followed by, "Like really? April 1st?" To which my smart mouth wants to reply, "Well duh! I just told you." Instead, I go for, "That's exactly right." I will save the details about our marriage for a later chapter. However, after our wedding, we immediately decided to try having a baby. There was no urgency, yet it was a priority to us, given that my husband is twenty-three years older than me. This concept of trying for a baby was quite foreign to me. Somewhere in my brain, I tucked away the idea that all it took for a baby to be conceived is a sexual act. In my mind, if you partook of that act without any contraceptives, you immediately became pregnant. This mindset made it extremely difficult for me to grasp the idea that couples were "trying" to have a baby. In my head, I always thought, "Just have sex!" Oh, how naïve I was. If it were that simple, then many women wouldn't carry the burden of not ever knowing what it is like to birth a biological child. And if you are a woman reading this who finds herself in this specific category, my heart goes out to you and it is my prayer that God, by the power of the Holy Spirit, comforts you and gives you peace. After birthing my own child and going through the process of pregnancy, you best believe I will never again utter or think of the words, "Just have sex!"

After my parents had Suzanne and me, I am assuming they wanted to expand our family. Of course neither one of them consulted me to see if by any chance after four years of being on earth, I was willing to give up my seat on the throne of youngest sibling. I guess my opinion didn't really matter since Suzanne didn't get a say in my birth either. I vaguely remember my mother's pregnancy with her third child. I am assuming I was suffering from betrayal. How dare my parents choose to expand the family? Wasn't I enough? Proverbs

16:18 states that "Pride comes before the fall," and sure enough, Deborah took my seat on the throne of youngest sibling. I remember her coming home, swaddled in a pink blanket and radiant. Her skin was as soft as the Johnson & Johnson babies on the commercials. She had a small face and was light skinned like Suzanne. I never understood how those two turned out light skinned when both of our parents were mocha rather than latte. However, the idea of being a big sister grew on me. I was eager to help my mom with anything baby related. In some instances, I took the motherly role very seriously. I felt accomplished when I helped and not being the youngest didn't seem bad after all. Having a baby in the house fulfilled my sudden curiosities. Questions such as, "What is in breast milk?" invaded my mind. "Does it taste like regular milk?" To which my mother gladly entertained by letting me suck on her breast one time as she was feeding Deborah. DISGUSTING! Having breastfed our third child and now understanding how breastfeeding and food intake go hand in hand, I often wonder what in the world my mother ate that day. Nevertheless, I vowed that I would never taste breast milk again. Some of you may be laughing at me at this point. But what can I say? No one had taught me to never say never. Sure enough, while on my breastfeeding journey, I tasted my own milk and cried any time I spilled the liquid gold after pumping. It didn't taste as bad as I remembered it. Who knows? Maybe I just eat more sweets than my mother did.

Maman made motherhood seem effortless. Though I always gave her a run for her money behaviorally, I never questioned whether Maman loved us. She exuded joy as she lived out her role as mom. Maman was relatively taller than Papa. Despite having given birth, she looked slim and had a glow about her. I remember the smile on her face as she cared for Deborah. After all, babies are simply adorable those first few months. My mind would prefer to remain in these magnificent moments, yet the reality of my relationship with pain is that Maman's smile faded with time. She went from enjoying Deborah's precious face to weeping over a casket. Within a few months of celebrating Deborah's arrival, our home was packed with friends and family offering their condolences. I was four years old and can vividly recall the scene as the crowd of people sang hymns while crying and lamenting as Deborah's casket was being carried to the cemetery. As a Congolese child, adults do not take time to explain to you what is going on. I love that my culture takes pride in shielding children from things, yet I know this methodology can be breeding ground for generational lies and secrets. It is unfortunate that I have yet to know what caused Deborah's death. It pains me that I will never know who she could have become, and it saddens me even more to acknowledge that pain had befriended me yet again. But this time, it was disguised as death.

Webster dictionary defines death as "a permanent cessation of all vital functions: the end of life." I quickly learned the permanence in Deborah's death as the somber days displayed on Maman's face felt like eternity. As a mother neither my heart nor my brain can reckon the emotional toll losing one of my children would have on me and it is my prayer that I never find out. The beauty however with death is that its antonym is life. In Genesis chapter 9, God blesses Noah after the flood and makes a covenant with him. Verses 13 through 16 states,

> I do set my bow in the cloud, and it shall be for a token of a covenant between me and the earth. And it shall come to pass, when I bring a cloud over the earth, that the bow shall be seen in the cloud: And I will remember my covenant, which is between me and you and every living creature of all flesh; and the waters shall no more become a flood to destroy all flesh. And the bow shall be in the cloud; and I will look upon it, that I may remember the everlasting covenant between God and every living creature of all flesh that is upon the earth. (KJV)

In these verses, God promises Noah that the rainbow will forever be a reminder of His covenant with every living creature. In this context, a rainbow becomes a symbol of hope, faithfulness, and joy after the storm. According to Google search, a rainbow baby is a child that is born after a miscarriage, stillbirth, or death by from natural causes, and for Maman, Naomi was just that.

Rebels Rebel

In the Bible, Naomi is first introduced in the book of Ruth. Ruth chapter 1 indicates that she is the wife of Elimelech, mother of Mahlon and Chilion, and mother-in-law of Ruth and Orpah. According to the Hebrew Interlinear Concordances, Strong's H5281, Naomi means "my delight." How fitting that after Deborah's death, Maman would give birth to another daughter and name her Naomi. I don't know if Maman knew the meaning of this name yet knowing what I know of my mother through her relatives, I have no doubt there was intentional thought behind her choice. It is difficult to recall Maman's pregnancy with Naomi. The two-year gap between Deborah's death and Naomi's birth is not vivid in my mind. What I do remember however, is how delightful it was to see Papa walk in the house to announce that our little sister had been born. One of my fondest memories with Suzanne is January 17th. We eagerly sat in our room waiting on Papa to come back from the hospital. As he walked into the hallway, we could barely hold ourselves still as the natural adrenaline pumped into our bloodstream at the thought of good news. Papa was a short and slender man. Given his profession, he was often serious and direct. Yet on this day, the professional walls seem to have come down and I saw a proud father. As Suzanne and I ran to hug him, he exclaimed, "Your sister was born this morning!" We were in his arms as he finished his sentence and before he took another breath, we jumped off him and ran to our room.

Suzanne and I were never allowed to jump on our beds. But I have learned as a parent now that occasionally, certain rules can be broken. As Naomi made her debut in the world, we celebrated being older sisters by jumping on the bed. Our beds were obviously not trampolines. However, in the minds of a ten and six years old, the thrill of breaking the rules along with a new life to celebrate made it seem as though they were. We must have been jumping for less than five minutes and…you guessed it! BOOM! Some part of the frame broke. I can't recall having to explain the phenomenon to Maman, nor is there a recollection of repercussion because of our action. Nonetheless, within a blink, the moment in which we were focused on joy turned into worrying. Though rules can be broken, we often pay a price in breaking protocol.

As a former English language learner, I couldn't be more appreciative that the Merriam Webster dictionary online offers definition of words in plain English for people whose first language is not English. Though I have spent more than a decade in the United States and have accumulated a few degrees, nothing irritates me like a convoluted definition. As I searched for the meaning of the word protocol, nothing satisfied my inquiry as much as the ELL (English Language Learner) definition, which defines protocol as: "a system of rules that explain the correct conduct and procedures to be followed in formal situations." Although it would be very hard to argue whether Suzanne and I demonstrated correct conduct in hearing the news about Naomi, no one can ever explain if the procedures Maman followed a few months into Naomi's birth were part of protocol.

The Democratic Republic of the Congo gained its independence from Belgium on June 30th, 1960. Given the current political state of the country, I struggle celebrating this day. While every country has its share of problems, the D.R.C., though rich in minerals, is considered one of the poorest countries in the world. The country gained its independence as the Republic of Congo and changed its name to Democratic Republic of the Congo in 1964 under the leadership of President Joseph Kasavubu. Upon his departure from office, President Joseph-Desire Mobotu took office and officially changed the country's name to Zaire in 1971. He ruled the country for 31 years! Talk about loving power. Upon overthrowing Mobutu in 1997, Laurent Desire Kabila changed the name back to Democratic Republic of the Congo. His reign did not last long, and he was overthrown by his son, Joseph Kabila, who has been in power since

2001. As mentioned before, I struggle celebrating Congo's independence because its history since 1960 shows no democracy or freedom for the people. Having lived in the United States and being taught how its government system works, it is very difficult for me to reconcile the idea of that which exists in the Congo as a functioning political system. I do acknowledge that I am by no means an expert on the affairs of the D.R.C. and would probably suffer long if attempted to understand it all. However, what I do know is that the country's turmoil in change of leadership the year Naomi was born altered my six-year-old heart from ever believing in superheroes.

When Laurent Desire Kabila became president in May of 1997, Naomi was exactly three months old, and Maman had barely been accustomed to her postpartum period. The entire country was anxious as a new political party took charge. Mobutu had been in power for over 30 years and the concept of him ever divorcing his bride, the Congo, was shocking to everyone, despite the consensus that it was needed. While God never intended for marriage to end in divorce, those who find themselves divorced, no matter how long they were married or how awful the marriage may have been, struggle to cope with the idea of moving forward through uncharted territories. While President Mobutu received treatment abroad between the year 1996 and 1997, the Alliance of Democratic Forces of the Liberation of Congo-Zaire (ADFL), a coalition of Rwandan, Ugandan, Burundian and selected Congolese dissidents worked tirelessly to capture various cities in the country until reaching the capital, Kinshasa. This tactic aided in putting out Mobutu and brought in President Laurent Kabila. Among the cities ravished by the rebels was Kananga where we lived. News had traveled through the country that the rebels were making their way through the country, traveling by car and foot, and that each town should be prepared for casualties, as these men had only one goal in mind—seize the country.

As a doctor in the town, Papa was considered one of the leaders in the Tshikaji community. In preparation for the rebels' arrival, a town meeting was called. Though every member of the town could not be at the meeting, the key leaders and some members of the community were present. The meeting was held in a house, and some key elements were discussed. I vaguely remember the details of what the meeting entailed. However, I do recall everyone acknowledging that Papa would be responsible for some keys, and no one was supposed to give out that information. Everyone left the meeting understanding that they should stock up on necessary provisions prior to the soldiers arriving in our town. As everyone frantically prepared, it all seemed like an action movie that would end soon. Of course, none of the adults took time to explain exactly why these rebels were coming to town. Yet we were expected to be cooperative without worry or questions.

In the Kasonga household, we began the long journey of packing most of our belongings and placing them in the attic. One by one, boxes with our most precious belongings went up with no concrete idea if we would see them again nor exactly when the rebels would arrive in our town. It was a quiet evening during the week and most of the people in the community were in their homes. News had traveled that the soldiers would be arriving to Tshikaji that same night. Because our town was small and population, the adults and leaders in the community predicted that the rebels would be passing through without causing long lasting damage. Nevertheless, being that the hospital where Papa worked had a storage area with gasoline, the rebels would more than likely stop to replenish and head on to their next destination. It dawned on me later that evening that the keys Papa was designated to have, were indeed the most important element that would stop the rebels on their track. Of course, everyone at the meeting vowed to not share where the keys were. Yet given the events that occurred later that evening, I quickly learned the truth in Matthew 5:37: "But let your 'Yes' be 'Yes,' and your 'No' be 'No.' For whatever is more than these is from the evil one." On the night of the meeting, it was easy for everyone to agree to keep Papa's identity hidden if there weren't any external pressures. But when a man threatens to kill your family if you don't give him what he needs, even the most well-intentioned human being will choose to protect their family regardless of the pain their decision may inflict on someone else.

With a newborn in the house and an aunt visiting, Maman attempted to make our days leading up to the soldiers' arrival as normal as possible. Suzanne and I played outside or entertained ourselves with the few toys that had not been put in the attic. The air outside smelled like fear and the temperature spelled out anxiety. As the evening came, we continued our habitual routine of dinner, showers and then bed. That night, however, was different. After dinner, Papa informed Maman that he needed to swing by the hospital to ensure everything was okay. Maman was obviously in disagreement with his plan and insisted that it was not safe to be out. Their interaction occurred with no fighting words and quite frankly, I can't recall ever witnessing them fighting in front of us. This is a practice I am intentionally growing to keep in our household. Though she expressed her disapproval, Papa's decision had been made. Maman's face looked disappointed, yet her body language, which I have now learned, yielded to the directive of the head of her household. She exemplified in that moment, submission. In my teens, I always heard that wives should submit to their husbands, but no one ever told me that it's harder to submit when you just can't support your husband's decision. And I couldn't stand the thought of being submissive to a wrong decision! My God, have I learned through my own marriage to respect God's biblical design of authority in marriage, with time of course and plenty of mistakes along the way. I have often wondered if Maman should have put her foot down so to say and not allowed Papa to go. Because that night I quickly realized that *in the absence of an earthly father's protection, his weakest vessels will be devoured.*

Papa said his goodbyes and left. Maman was listening to a worship music cassette as she watched Naomi sleep in the bassinette. Suzanne decided that it was a good time for her to shower while I sat at the dining room table with my aunt wishing this night could be over. Then there was a knock at the door. "DO NOT OPEN YOUR DOORS" was the protocol given at the community meeting weeks before. “AND WHAT IF THEY SHOOT THROUGH THE DOOR?” someone asked. No concrete answer was given. So, when the knock came to our door, Maman fearlessly walked and peeped to see who it was. The rebels had arrived. She had two choices. To open or not to open, that was the question. Yet before she could properly analyze the situation,

“We know you’re in there,” one man said. “Open this door!”

Maman opened the door, and I could see men standing in green uniforms holding guns.

“Where is Dr. Kasonga?” the man in charge questioned.

“My husband is not here, and I do not know when he will return,” Maman responded calmly.

“We need the hospital keys, RIGHT NOW!” the rebel shouted.

“Officer, we do not have any keys and I don’t even know what you are talking about,” Maman responded. While the conversation happened, the other soldiers were circulating the house. Then a voice from the back said,

“Since you don’t know where the keys are, we will come in and search for them ourselves! Now, move out of our way.”

Maman stepped to the side and let the men enter our home. I remember hating my father in that moment and questioning if he loved us. How could he leave us behind knowing these ruthless rebels were ravishing anything that stood in the way of their mission? I immediately ran from the dining room table to the kitchen, attempting to hide behind the door. As their commander gave orders to look through our belongings, my aunt, Naomi, Maman and I stood there helpless.

“All clear!” said one soldier.

“All clear!” said the next one. With a disappointed look in his eye, the commander looked at Maman and said,

"Turn that worship music off right now. There is nothing your God can do for you. As a matter of fact, we're taking that radio with us."

Maman unplugged the radio and sarcastically responded, "I told you we don't have any keys."

"On second thought," the commander added, "soldiers, please take any and everything you see that you want!"

As someone who loved karate movies and superheros, my heart sunk. This is the time when I needed superpowers. The bad guys I had once seen in movies causing harm were now in our sanctuary and I could not do anything. I stood by the door nervous, swallowing saliva in silence pretending I couldn't be seen. I whispered in my heart, "God, if you are real, please do something." Everyone said God is omniscient, and I could not reconcile the idea that an all knowing and loving God could possibly see what was happening in our home and not intervene. And before I could finish my hope for a Savior, I heard Maman say, "Can't you see I have a newborn baby? Can't you see I have a family? Who is supposed to care for them?" Without a care in his eye, the commander ordered his soldiers to take Maman with them. Maman did not resist the order. She put her shoes on and did not even look back to say goodbye. Maybe she knew something I did not know. But I will never know. Hot tears streamed down my face as the painful internal groaning of my soul was ready to erupt. I watched Maman close the doors as the soldiers laughed, demonstrating no pity. I clung to my aunt and unlike the plane experience from Ivory Coast to the Congo, my mother was being taken away from me. The chatter seemed to diminish as the seconds lasted for what felt like eternity. Suddenly, I heard a big BANG! Though I had never had any experience with guns, I knew I heard gunshots. My aunt and I dropped to our knees in anguished screaming, "NOOOOOOOOOOOOOOOOOOO!" Suzanne who had been taking a shower through the entire ordeal ran out in a towel to see what had just happened. Neither my aunt nor I had any words to fully explain what had just happened.

Just as fast as the tears rolled down our cheeks, a screaking sound came from the front door. Maman walked in untouched, at least from what we could see. She hugged us all and said the rebels walked away with her, shot in the air to scare her, and then let her go because she was useless to them. There was a sense of relief for a moment and at the same time we were all concerned for Papa's safety. We sat in our now stripped living room silently mortified while awaiting Papa's arrival. Would he ever return? I thought, or would his life be traded for gasoline?

There came a second knock on the door. This time, Maman did not seem confident walking to see who it was.

"Who is it?" Maman asked.

"It's me," a man responded. It sounded like Papa's voice, but Maman looked through the peephole and saw Papa standing there having no clue what had just occurred in his absence to his wife and children. With a sense of relief, Maman opened the door and gave Papa the disappointing wife look and even at six years old, I knew it would be a long night. Maman carefully explained to Papa what had happened and made sure to express that we could no longer stay in our house until we knew for sure the rebels had left Tshikaji. The Bible says that "weeping may endure for a night, but joy comes in the morning" (Psalm 30:5), yet no one accurately expresses how long a night may be. That night I slept petrified by the thought of having to run outside after those gun shots and see Maman lying there dead. I could not sleep, and my heart raced throughout the night, weeping at the thought of death, while hoping joy would soon make a debut.

The morning eventually did come. We packed the few belongings we had left and travelled to a nearby village. I had heard of huts made from sand and seen them in pictures, but never had I imagined making such a place home indefinitely. We were welcomed by people who Papa knew and shown where we would be staying. I couldn't help but state the obvious. "Everyone looks like a villager," I whispered to Suzanne.

"And exactly where do you think we are?" she answered sarcastically.

"This is a village Njiba!" I immediately knew based on her response that she was not in the mood and based on how quiet Maman had been that day, I was certain she had no energy for my habitual shenanigans. We carefully laid out our mats made with palm leaves and stayed indoors for the next three days. Three days later, we received word that the rebels had left our town and it was safe to return. A sigh of relief perfumed the atmosphere. Papa thanked the people who hosted us, and we gladly returned to the home we knew. I realized there were many things in our home I had taken for granted such as beds, food, light, entertainment, air conditioning and the list could go on. Upon our arrival into Tshikaji, the community was celebrating the departure of the rebel with songs and praises to God. Though their weeping endured for a night, joy did come. I outwardly participated in the festivities and inwardly mourned that a part of my innocence had been stripped away. During our three days in the village, I couldn't tell you what we ate, what conversation we had or exactly how I felt during that time. *There are moments in our lives that are very traumatic in nature, and yet we choose to place them in the recess of our minds.* Almost losing Maman, not because I couldn't open an airplane bathroom door, but at the hands of vile men who had weapons of destruction, created an aching in my heart that I never wanted to feel again. So, I dumped the memory as far as my brain cells could. At least this way I didn't have to face the fact that humanity is sinful, and the heart of man is evil. Left unto itself, it will always rebel.

The Truth

A few months after our encounter with the rebels, Papa received a promotion at the hospital. He would now be overseeing others in his department and have an increase in responsibility. Though more responsibility does not always equate to better pay, we were blessed to have an increased income and a better home located in another part of the city known as Kananga II. The house we would be living in was inhabited by a Caucasian couple whose responsibilities Papa was now inheriting. I was excited to be leaving Tshikaji. While I had some fond memories there, losing Deborah and having rebels visit us were enough to want a new scenery.

Our new house was bigger than our old one. It reminded me of the Garden of Eden. The grass was green and there were trees planted all over the yard. We had lemons, bananas, guava, and grapes. We had a field in the front where we planted peanuts, sugar cane, cassava leaves and other vegetables. The layout of the backyard allowed us to raise different animals, such as goats, sheep, or chickens. The yard was huge and gated with brick walls. As a girl who couldn't sit still, the house had so much space for me to run around. With a bigger home, we needed more helpers. Maman hired a security guard, a kitchen maid, a laundry maid, and a chauffeur. Looking back, it amazes me how good we had it for people who lived in what is considered one of the poorest countries in the world. While I knew and saw poor people around me daily, my parents afforded us a lifestyle that I have yet to be able to give my own children.

After the events in our old home, I couldn't help but live in expectancy for the greatest memories to be made in the new house. Though it seemed like pain had been befriending me for my entire life thus far, I was eager for a fresh start and even had a desire to believe in something greater than myself. Yes, the invasion of the rebels allowed me to see that movie superheroes weren't real, but for some reason, calling a place that resembled the Garden of Eden "home" caused me to dream again. Dreams are defined as a series of thoughts, images and sensations occurring in a person's mind during sleep. But daydreaming is a series of pleasant thoughts that distract one's attention from the present. Somehow, from a young age, I became acquainted with both types of dreams. I dreamed and still dream on a regular basis. Though I cannot always remember every dream, there are vivid ones that stay with me forever, no matter how big or small they may seem to other people. I used to shy away from telling people my dreams because of the responses I would get. But I have grown to know when my dreams are from the Lord, from a multitude of business or demonic. Ecclesiastes 5:3 states, "For a dream cometh through the multitude of business," indicating that sometimes the series of thoughts and images we see while we are sleeping derive from things we have done throughout the day. For example, you could watch a movie with a scene of people being chased and that night you dream that you are being chased. The scenes are similar, and you almost experience a déjà vu.

I remember one morning waking up and rushing to my closet. Unlike many young girls around me, I did not enjoy playing with Barbie. I would cut her hair and attempt to make her play basketball. So, for many occasions, I often asked for toy cars. I had recently received a toy race car. It was red with black lines. The wheels were shining, and it was one of my most valuable toys. I played with it so much when I got it and could imagine myself racing in it. Though this dream may have been because of my own imagination, one night I vividly recall dreaming that my body had shrunk and that I was somehow able to get into the toy car. My dream was so real to me that I expected to find myself with the ability to drive when I woke up. Yet to my biggest disappointment, the race car was in the closet exactly where I had left it and I was still young with no ability to drive. I stood there confused. How is this possible? The events were so real to me. When I shared my dream with Maman, she laughed.

"Not long ago, you woke up in the morning with your pants on your arms because you were having some dream. Another time, you woke up and got ready for school because you were dreaming so hard and thought it was the next day. Now you want to tell me about some race car experience? You have the most bizarre dreams." Talk about words of encouragement! Of course, I chucked it off like I didn't care. Truthfully, I wanted someone to believe me and if Maman didn't, I knew no one else would. From then on, I became reluctant to share with anyone the series of images that would cross my mind, whether they were in a daydream or in a dream while I was sleeping. So, I grew to not pay attention to them. Yet there was a dream or almost a vision that I have held onto for many years.

In 2 Corinthians 12, Paul talks about the revelations that God shows him and in verse 3 it states, "I know a man in Christ who fourteen years ago was caught up to the third heaven. Whether it was in the body or out of the body I do not know—God knows." One night, after the usual bedtime routine and fighting sleep, I eventually fell asleep. Like Paul, as I recall the events, it is difficult for me to say whether this experience was in the body or out of the body, God knows. But what I do know is that this dream is still as real to me as when it happened more than twenty years ago. As I laid in bed, a bright and shining light entered my room. I saw the silhouette of what I knew to be a man. He was dressed in white and His face I could not see. There was warmth and joy in His presence. The man did not say anything to me, but He seemed pleased with me. I grew up going to church and had heard about Jesus though I did not have a relationship with Christ. Without anyone's counsel, I knew that this man was Jesus. I even referred to Him by the name Jesus. Our interaction was brief, and the light diminished from my bedroom. I quickly rose and followed the light. I know I couldn't possibly know for sure who this man was, why He came to my room or where He was headed now. But I knew I did not want Him to leave. As I raced behind Him, He made His way to the front lawn of our house. The grass looked greener than it typically did and every tree around was lit because of the light coming from this man. His back was facing me, and I yelled, "Jesus! Don't leave me. Take me with you, please!" The man turned around and while I couldn't see His face, I sensed the warmth of a loving father and friend. He reached out His hand as to motion for me to come closer. I walked towards Him, and He began to ascend to the sky. As tears flowed down my face, I heard His voice say, "Your time has yet to come. I will come back for you. You are still needed here." While those words may have been comforting, I was in distress. How could Jesus visit me and not take me with Him? I immediately woke up, confused why I was still on my bed. I rushed outside to the spot where I was last standing, praying that I would find the man there. To my greatest regret, there was not light nor a man. I stood there amazed wondering if anyone else had seen the light that night. Yet because of being rejected previous times, I thought it was better to not even ask.

As much as I had wished someone would validate my dream, I had had enough painful experiences to know that no one would. This became the breeding ground for struggles with rejection. As I grew older, I had to unlearn the idea that people's rejection of my thoughts, ideas or even experiences wasn't necessarily a rejection of my being. And if it was, I had to learn to be secure in the truth of God's word: "I am fearfully and wonderfully made" (Psalm 139:14). Needless to say, amid knowing my dream would be nullified and I would be made fun of for once again having bizarre dreams, I held on to the man in the light dream because it gave me hope. Hope that there was a Savior. Hope that my pain could be temporary. Hope that one day He would be true to His promise and come for me. Hope that there was a reason why He did not let me go with Him. I knew not His name, nor was I interested to name Him. In my dream, I called Him Jesus and knew in my heart of hearts that He was. Yet with a life not surrendered to Jesus Christ, what was once a vivid dream became a fleeting thought. The reality of my circumstances gave no room for me to daydream. If there was ever a Savior, His intervention would have been greatly appreciated.

CHAPTER 3: FOR BETTER, FOR WORSE

In Sickness and in Health

A year and some months later after Naomi's birth and after we had already moved into our new house, we found out that Maman was pregnant again. This time I did not feel offended by their choice to expand the family because Maman was carrying two little humans in her belly. The thought and excitement of getting two little siblings for the price of one pregnancy excited me. Of course, I had no idea at the time what it means to be pregnant for nine months and now having gone through the process, God bless Maman for enduring that pregnancy. From the first trimester, she was always tired, throwing up and losing weight. She was not eating much and lost hair. I thought these symptoms were strange, but I associated them with needing more energy to carry two people. As the pregnancy progressed, we found out that Maman was having a boy and a girl. I was thrilled at the idea of finally having a little brother who could run wild with me. Like many children awaiting their siblings, I repeatedly asked when the babies would be here. Though my excitement increased, Maman's health seemed to decrease. More and more she would spend a good portion of the day lying down on the floor or in her bedroom. It was as if all the adults knew what was going on and I didn't.

I distinctly remember a few months prior to the twin's arrival, Maman had a friend who was a prayer warrior. Her friend came over one night, and they began to intercede for Mama's healing. I remember Maman worshipping, crying and praying at the top of her lungs. This was the first time I had seen her with this much energy in months. We were in the living room, but I don't recall Papa being present. As she and her friend prayed, Maman was fired up. She began to run in circles in the living room and pray in a tongue that was unknown to me. It didn't sound like any of the languages I had heard her speak before. She was alive, vibrant, confident, and it seemed as though a shift had occurred. Eventually the days and months passed. On April 2, 1999, Maman gave birth to my youngest siblings, Nathan, and Anna. Just like Naomi's birth, Papa came home to tell us of the news of their arrival. Except this time, he did not have only good news. He said that Maman and our siblings had to stay in the hospital for a few more days before they could come home. Though disappointed, I waited patiently.

Shortly after, Maman and the twins were released. Customary to many African households, we had family and friends over to celebrate their arrival. We praised God, danced, ate, drank and were merry. I watched Nathan's and Anna's faces soak in their new environment. They were so tiny, Anna more than Nathan. Furthermore, they were beautiful. I admit that I may have been biased. However, I thought they were the cutest little people. Unfortunately, as quickly as people had gathered at our house to celebrate the twin's birth, we ended up having another gathering soon after. Within the next couple weeks, Maman was not feeling any better and was taken back to the hospital. Not one person explained to us what was happening or what she was suffering of. Thankfully Maman was at the hospital Papa worked at. He would see her during the day and then come home to be with us. In his absence, our maids would take care of us. One Saturday Papa came back after visiting Maman and told us that we wouldn't go to church the next day. Maman had requested to see us because she missed us. Suzanne and I were elated to be able to see her. I missed having her around. Though only eight years old, I knew a home should have both parents in it. That night I barely closed my eyes and was up before Papa could even wake us up. Suzanne and I were dressed waiting for Papa in the living room as he took his shower. Suddenly, there was a knock on the door.

Suzanne opened the door and to our biggest surprise, one of Papa's younger brothers was standing there with a few other men. Their stance was awkward, and their countenance did not seem pleasing. My uncle then asked if Papa was around, and we told him he was in the shower. My uncle asked me to go tell Papa there were some people here for him. I ran to the shower, knocked, and yelled through the door, "Your brother is here." Papa told me to inform them that he would be out shortly. We stood there waiting for Papa to come out, while none of the adults engaged us in conversation. When Papa had finished getting dressed, he walked out to the living room. As soon as he made eye contact with his brother and saw the people who had come with him, he knew. He fell to the ground and let out a big groan. I looked at Suzanne for any sign of understanding and a voice in the room said, your mom died last night.

I couldn't believe what my ears were hearing. Maman had promised she would come back. She had prayed and asked for healing. She was a good person and a good mom. How could God take her? I was in disbelief and unfortunately, the adults in my family do not value communicating with children about anything. They raised us with a "do as I say and not as I do" mentality. They engrained in us that we were not their friends. We were beneath them and were not privileged to the information they had. While they may have never fully wanted to utter what I have just written, this is how it felt to be left out of the conversation. This was our mom after all, and no one cared to tell us exactly what had happened. Within an hour, we were taken to another relative while Papa and the adults attempted to figure out funeral plans.

Having endured many funerals, I am now familiar with how quickly things happen. Within that week there was a scheduled "matanga"—mourning day—at our house. Unlike the processes in the U.S., somehow Maman's body was able to come to our house. I remember our living room being dismantled so we could fit the many people that would come. Papa being known in the community increased the amount of traffic our house would get. I watched Maman's casket being laid on the floor. She looked at peace and she was beautiful. Everyone in the room was crying and I couldn't get myself to produce a tear. I chose to tell myself I was dreaming. I would wake up and Maman would still be around. However, every once in a while, in the midst of wishing I was in a dream, I would overhear people talking about Maman.

There were many theories floating around as possibilities and even today I still don't know why and how Maman died. Some said she had complications delivering the twins and lost a lot of blood—this is one I have used often because I truly don't know what to tell people. Others said that Papa contracted AIDS because he slept with a lady during one of his medical missions and then gave it to Maman, which made her susceptible to death. And the best one was that we her children were witches and sacrificed her for something. I am not sure what shocked me more, the fact that Maman was dead, or the accusations made concerning her death. The saddest part was that these things were being said by people who weren't outsiders but rather other family members. Unfortunately, at eight years old, I had no voice or power to defend myself or my family. I kept my mouth shut and pretended all these people would soon disappear and my life would be back to normal. I was sadly mistaken. My life would never go back to normal, and I regret not mourning Maman while I could still touch her physical body. I never got the chance to say goodbye. I never allowed myself to cry, and now as I look back, I will always wonder if her absence from the body means she is present with the Lord.

Till Death Do Us Part

When a man and a woman get married and express their vows to each other, neither of them envisions being separated by death. Yet this was the reality for Papa. How was he supposed to pick up his life once again now that his bride was no longer with him? Many people believe that men are less to show their emotions, and there is some truth to that because many men tend to lean on logic rather than sentiment. However, you will never see a more broken man than an unexpected widower. When I look at my son Tito, I see my father's smile. It's a smile I recognize simply because I last saw it in 1999 prior to Maman's passing.

With maids, guards and chauffeurs in place, Papa was still able to go to work while we went to school. He made sure he was home for dinner. We still went to church on Sundays and visited our nearest family members. But something had changed. Papa did not have any pep in his steps. He seemed lifeless and he ate less. He had been serious most times, but now he barely cracked a smile. At eight years old I couldn't have imagined what he may have been feeling and the thoughts that ran through his mind as he mourned his beloved wife.

The first year without mom happened like a blur and there were a couple events within that year that bothered me. For months, I noticed that Papa's strength had been diminishing. Having witnessed Maman suffer through her pregnancy with the twins, I was not sure what to think as I saw the signs. Yet Papa continued to work and play his part as father, brother and doctor. Then one Sunday, we all went to church like we normally would. While in the middle of singing songs, I watched Papa collapse on the floor and the entire congregation take a big gasp of air. An uncle and a few men rushed to his rescue. I couldn't see anything else. We ended up leaving the service and were later told that Papa was diabetic, and his sugar was low. Being that there are other diabetics on Papa's side of the family, it's a compelling argument. It was just hard to believe, and it is still a hard pill to swallow since Papa never had an issue before.

Life went on and we were able to move past the church episode. Then something else happened that caused me to question exactly what was happening with Papa's health. Papa was spending more days at home than at work. One day as I looked at his pile of dirty clothes, I noticed that many of his undergarments were soaked in blood. I was puzzled. Was Papa peeing blood continually or just sick that one day? I went to the male maid who washed his clothes and asked him why Papa's clothes were soaked in blood. I am not sure what I expected as a response, but the maid told me it was impolite to look at Papa's draws and that I should mind my own business.

Consequently, I minded my business. I went to school like a typical 4th grader should. I played with my friends at school and competed to be the very best in everything. Somewhere in the trenches of it all I somehow forgot that Maman had been gone for almost a year and that Papa had been adjusting to it. He didn't disclose how he felt to us, and he left us clueless about his health. One day, Papa left for work like he typically would. That night we got word that he would be working late, and we shouldn't stay up waiting for him. Like obedient kids, we went to bed. The next morning, Suzanne and I woke up for school. There was a male relative who lived with us who made sure we were transported to school by our driver. As we arrived at our drop off location, a gentleman recognized our vehicle and the relative who lived with us. Suzanne and I were sitting in the back of the van. As our relative opened the door, the gentleman came in a hurry and seemed to have something important to share.

"Man, you haven't heard? Dr. Kasonga died this morning!" he yelled passionately.

Our relative had a look of disbelief and immediately cautioned the man that he had kids in the back. Before the man could take his cue, he uttered, "They announced it on the radio this morning. Everyone in the town knows." Our relative motioned us to get out as if we had not heard the news. Somehow, he wanted us to pretend everything was okay. I chose to do just that. I walked myself to school as I saw people in the street looking at me with eyes of pity. I overheard different people wondering if we knew our father had died. We kept walking anyways. When I arrived at school, the director immediately called for a time a prayer. In her address to the students, she asked that everyone pray for my family and me as we mourn the loss of our father, Dr. Kasonga.

For some reason as I heard her say those words, it immediately dawned on me that the Dr. Kasonga everyone was referencing was not some stranger I had never met. This was my father. This was the guy who had gone to work yesterday and told me he would see me later. This is the man whom I had always admired and wanted to be like.

This man whom I had the pleasure of calling Papa was gone, and I did not even get to say goodbye. Like a rushing wind, groaning overflowed my belly, and the flood gates of tears were opened. My Papa was gone. Only a year since Maman had left and nobody had an explanation for it. My protector and my covering I would no longer see. My heart ached with questions that no one was willing to answer. Today I still have many questions left unanswered. My husband, Dr. Tito Tirado, once preached and asked a rhetorical question to the congregations stating, "Can you live with a question mark?"

There were no words to express the pain of losing Papa. It felt unreal. He was not only my father, but he had helped many people in the community through optometry. The entire town felt his absence, and now looking back I still wonder if he and my mother were religious people, or had they secured eternity with God by accepting Christ as their Lord and Savior? I will never know in this lifetime, and I am choosing to trust that God who is all knowing knows better than I do. Nevertheless, in the heat of my pain, I vowed to myself that I would honor Papa by becoming an optometrist and never questioned if that was what God intended for my life. I later learned that *when not properly managed, pain will cause us to make decisions birthed out of flesh.*

The Unpardonable Sin

It was time to readjust with no full understanding of what had happened those last two years. Suzanne was 13, Naomi 3, the twins 1, me 9, and we were officially orphans. Naomi and the twins had no idea what was happening and no one in the family would ever take the time to explain to them how drastic their lives would be changing. Papa's funeral was a big event in the town of Kananga. Many of his family members traveled to come, including his brother from the United States, who would later adopt us through the Congolese government.

As people continued to mourn, Papa's siblings met and decided our fate. It was determined that all five of us would go stay with one of our uncles who also lived in Kananga. He and his wife had five kids of their own, plus us would make a house of twelve. We were all around the same age and the adults believed it would be the best place for us to be while we awaited traveling to the United States. Since our uncle in the United States had six kids of his own who were mostly adults, he and his wife decided it wouldn't be wise for them to also take the twins. The twins were to stay with the cousins in Kananga, while Suzanne and I would go to the U.S. and Naomi's fate had yet to be determined. We packed our belongings and went to my uncle's house. Though I had interacted with them most of my young life, their household ran completely different than ours. I was tremendously sad because I was being forced to call these people mom and dad, but unlike Naomi and the twins I knew for a fact they were not my parents. I hated the fact that no one wanted to talk about Papa and Maman. The subject seemed taboo as if we were to just pretend, they had never existed.

As a very opinionated and free-spirited person, I had already made a deal with my own parents when it came to school in first grade. I had asked that they wouldn't be helicopter parents when it came down to academics and that I would always bring home good grades. If I broke that promise, then they could start checking my homework. Well, I always brought home good grades and never worried about being asked about school. Papa and Maman trusted me in that area and gave me the autonomy to make my own decisions. They gave me the freedom to negotiate with them and instilled in me confidence. But all that changed in the new environment. My uncle's wife had trained her kids with homework checks and other rules that I was just not down for. I had no choice and no voice whatsoever. I felt trapped and suffocated. I had a roof over my head, food, clothes and people around me, which I am forever grateful for. But as my husband says, "Even prisoners in America get that!"

Out of the five cousins, I was closer to the one girl who was around my age but was younger than me. The other two were way younger than me and the oldest two were obviously older than me.

Congolese culture prides itself for the hierarchal structure they enforce within the family. You are expected to reverence and respect your elders, which I have no problem with. What I cannot stand though is when those who are older use that as a tactic to infuse fear and manipulate the relationship. Sadly, this was my experience in that house. The mistreatment went from me being stuck doing the chores and getting the silent treatment from all the kids, to having my head shoved in a big tank of water as I screamed for help attempting to get some air. Enduring these things was not the toughest part. What made it hard was being told that my parents were dead, and I had no one to run to. That even if I snitched, no one would believe me. Hearing these words made me hate humanity and destructed my understanding of family. How could people who called themselves my relatives and shared part of my DNA treat me like this? To quote my husband, I have now learned that "DNA does not make you family" (Dr. Tito Tirado).

The family lines became blurry over time not only with the habitual verbal and physical abuse, but with two events that have changed me for as long as I live. The first happened as one of the older female cousins was talking to me about a sex scene she had seen in a movie. In her failed attempt to make me understand the scene, she forced me to lay down on the bed. I found it quite strange, but I was curious. She then laid herself on top of me and started to dry-hump me. I felt violated and knew this wasn't right. So, I quickly removed myself and reluctantly said I understood. That day, I felt as if a part of my innocence had been tainted.

Within a few months, our family of twelve moved into another part of town in the house Papa had started building before his death. I was sad to see that Papa and Maman didn't get to witness their dream house being completed and habitable. I knew they had goals and aspirations as they began building it. All this was no longer important. Nonetheless, I was thankful we had more space in the new house. As everyone got acquainted to the neighborhood and their new rooms, I became familiar with hands that woke me up in the middle of the night.

It started one afternoon while everyone was outside playing. He and I were inside because he summoned me to come. I have honestly forced myself to forget the details that led me to no longer call him my cousin because the pain he inflicted on me deemed him as my abuser. While in the house that day, he told me I was beautiful and that he liked me. His eyes were fixed on my nine-year-old body, and it's sickening to think he saw something that aroused him. He was only thirteen, yet I felt like a grasshopper facing a giant. He looked paranoid and in a hurry. He didn't want anyone to catch him. He forcefully planted his lips on mine attempting to kiss me passionately. He was taller and stronger than me. Internally, I was screaming for help. Externally, I was frozen. Though I said no, he took my hand and slowly moved it towards his private part. I couldn't help but wonder why I was touching a body part that felt like a rock. Maman had not lived long enough to give me proper lessons on sexual education, and I had no idea what was happening before me. Suddenly, someone came into the house, and he couldn't finish his conquest. His eyes pierced mine and he held my hand tighter than he ever had. He commanded me to not say anything to anyone and threatened to physically spank me.

At the age of nine, many of us come to understand right and wrong. Even when we have not been taught that a specific thing is essentially wrong, there is something innate in us that understands that something like being touched inappropriately is not acceptable. I was not sure what to do or think after the incident with my cousin, so I did what he required of me. I chose not to tell anyone. As much as I wished the first time would be the last, it was actually the beginning of what lasted for the next three years. He would come to the girls' room at night and wake me up by caressing my leg. Like a programmed machine, I would wake up and go to his room. He would start with kissing and moving my hand to touch his erected penis. Then he would tell me how much he loved me and that he should prove his love by inserting his penis into my vagina. At nine, I had never had anything penetrate my private area and I distinctively remember making grimaces as I held my scream internally so I wouldn't wake up anyone. I would lay there as he did his deed and came to a place of satisfaction. I just wanted it to end, and in my head, I would create all types of scenarios of him getting caught. We never did get caught, and like a T.V. on mute, I never made a sound to alert anyone.

Within a few months from the first time my cousin sexually abused me and raped me, I could not come to terms with calling him my cousin. He became a despicable creature who was sent from hell to make my life more miserable than it had already been for the last two years. Being the outspoken kid that I was, I decided that his behavior was not acceptable, and it was time to tell the adults. I conjured up the boldness to express to his parents that he was molesting me and having sex with me in the middle of the night. Surprisingly, when asked, he denied all my accusations. In return, I got whooped fiercely for "lying." I couldn't believe he could lie to his parents' face, watch me get punished and still have the nerve to look at me like a piece of meat. I knew then that I no longer had a voice. Telling the truth was not enough because no one believed me. I understood that day that it would always be his word against mine and if I lived with them, I would never win. Though I knew it was wrong and I felt ashamed of my existence in allowing him to make me the object of his sexual desires, every time he beckoned for me, I went. I went angry. I went humiliated. I went ashamed. I went hopeless. I went because this had become the norm. No one in the house cared to know how I was doing or to investigate if I was indeed telling the truth. No one cared and so I chose not to care. I numbed myself to the pain. I hardened my heart to the still small voice inside that said this was a sin and in doing so, a cycle of sexual perversion was birthed.

CHAPTER 4: THE LAND OF THE FREE

D.R.C. to U.S.A.

"You're going to the United States!" a relative announced to Suzanne and me shortly after the death of Papa. Papa came from a big family and according to the patriarchal Muluba customs, when parents died, the children belonged to the father's side. I have never dug to understand the reasoning of this tradition. However, I can make an educated guess that it stems from the ideology of traditional wedding. Customarily in the Democratic of Congo, the family of the man getting married pays a dowry to the family of his future wife during what is known as "marriage coutumier." When the dowry requested by the women's side is received, in the eyes of custom and culture, the couple is officially married. The woman can now live with the guy as her husband and bear children, and they can live their lives as a married couple. This is such a foreign concept to the western world, although in the western world we see couples choosing to cohabit without the formality of a civil or religious ceremony. So just like that, the fate of my siblings and I would now lie in the hands of other people.

When Papa and Maman were alive, we heard about this great country called the United States. It was portrayed as the "land of milk and honey." I however can't remember ever coveting being in this country. All my needs were met and as long as I could play outside, I was pretty satisfied. Papa had a brother who lived in the U.S. with his wife and kids. We saw Papa's brother when he came periodically. I distinctively recall even crying one time as his brother left after Deborah's funeral to head back for the United States. I can't say I wanted to go with him nor that I was emotionally invested in his presence. All I knew was that it made me sad to see him come and go. According to his memory, the image of me crying at his departure broke his heart and he promised himself he would come back for me. Well, he did keep his promise. Shortly after the funerals in Kananga,

Suzanne, Naomi, and I departed for Kinshasa, the capital of Congo. I was finally going to be able to see snow! I had read about snow in books, seen snow in pictures and heard all about it. But now, I was finally going to be in the land where white stuff magically falls from the sky when it's cold.

Though this was a major thrill, a part of me was also intrigued by how the United States would look. Plus, with most of the Congolese population living in poverty, saying you were heading to the U.S. gave you bragging rights. But all this excitement ceased when I heard devastating news. Because no one anticipated that both Papa and Maman would die, the responsibility of caring for all five of us would be too much for just one person. So the elders of Papa's family decided that it would be wise for us to be split. Suzanne was guided to a paternal uncle in Lumbubashi. Nathan and Anna at only one had no say in the matter and stayed with another paternal uncle in Kananga. While Naomi and I had the privilege to be taken to what I once believed was the promised land. However, I could no longer envision a land of milk and honey when I discovered that my abuser would be coming along. How dare the family allow this to happen? I was angry. I was bitter. I was tormented. I knew this meant no end to the rape and molestation. I did not know who to turn to and I internalized the pain. After all, what adult listens to a ten-year-old who can sometime have a smart mouth and would look at you sideways without thinking twice? But all that internal bravery did me no good. I shrunk. I felt worthless. I felt helpless. I had made the mistake of telling the truth once and no one believed me. Why would me saying, "NO! He can't come. He comes to my room at night and forcefully has sex with me!" be enough to stop the train that was already in motion? There was nothing I could do. He knew it too. So, when the news was announced that he would be coming, he looked at me with a smirk, as if to say, "You thought you were getting away, but you thought wrong!" Despite what may have been going on internally, I learned to mask the pain. This was the beginning of learning to cope with reality by living a double life. In the eyes of everyone, I should have been happy to go the U.S. I should have been grateful for a relative wanting to adopt me and take me to the U.S. But internally, I was resentful. The reason, they chose for him to come was simply a family trade off. The one paternal uncle who would be keeping the twins either asked or it was arranged for at least one of his kids to come to the US. And out of the five kids, the lot fell on my abuser.

The process of coming to the United States was not as easy as my paternal uncle thought it would be. They were first tasked to become American citizens to make the process easier and attempt to finalize adoption papers in the Congo. The Congo part took no time as the country breathes corruption and paying someone enough money will cause even the most fabricated documents to come to life. So, for one year, Naomi and I waited in Kinshasa with another paternal uncle. We lived with other cousins, and it's safe to say, from my lenses, our stay was the beginning of me feeling like I didn't belong. All our relatives obliged us to call our paternal uncles "dad" and wives "mom," while deep down my heart ached for my Papa and Maman. The sad part was that no one talked about them and acknowledged them as our parents. No one explained to us who they were beyond the tunnel vision that we had as kids. It was as if we were to pretend that they never existed and that all of a sudden, these relatives on my dad's side were the best thing since sliced bread. With Suzanne gone to Lumbubashi, there were many days when I was the recipient of family injustices. The injustice resembled anything from withholding food or simply being verbally abused. This quickly became my norm, and I never knew the covering my parents had provided us until they were no longer there.

There was however, one good thing out of that year. My abuser did not live with us! He was sent to live with a paternal aunt as we awaited traveling to America. Amid mourning Papa and Maman, not having him around was definitely one of the greatest highlights after my parents' death. If I had to choose between being hungry, homeless or being in his presence, I would have chosen hunger and homelessness on any given day. Yet despite him being physically away from me, he still visited where I lived. I avoided making eye contact or any interactions with him. Nonetheless, he found ways to look at me with seductive eyes and had a smirk that grosses me out to this day. At least he wasn't forcing me to have sex with him. That's what I had to keep telling myself.

The academic year went by rather quickly and unfortunately the process for us to come to America was yet to be finalized. This led to a decision made by the paternal uncles that Naomi, my abuser and I should go back to Kananga. The cost of living was cheaper than being at the capital and my uncle who took care of Nathan and Anna was in a better position to provide for all of us. With grief in my heart, we made the journey back to Kananga and waited for another year. It was another year of being ridiculed and sexually used by someone whom I had to present to the world as my brother. Another year of one of his siblings being the alpha female and dispensing demeaning monologues directed towards me. I had lost hope of ever landing on the soil of freedom. My heart ached bitterly inside my chest, and I cried silently with no one to tell.

I was told that because the Muluba culture is a patriarchal culture, the siblings of my father were to be referred to as Papa_____ or Maman ____. There is this notion that the children belong to the dad's family anyways and therefore, any of the father's siblings are your mom and dad, and not your aunt and uncle. The title aunt and uncle were reserved for the siblings of the mother. To be frank, I have never been fond of this tradition. While I appreciate the concept of respecting elders, over the years, it made me feel as though everyone around us wanted the existence of my parents to be nonexistent. Because people outside of my nuclear family and siblings are not aware of me telling my story through this book, I am refraining from citing individual names to protect their identity as best as I can. So, for the sake of keeping the story clear, I will refer to my paternal uncle and his wife who brought us to America as my adoptive parents.

Eventually the seconds became minutes that turned into hours and then days and months, and then it was time to go. We were told to pack light because this time around, Kinshasa would be a temporary stop. I packed a small green suitcase with a few items to last me one week. We said our goodbyes and traveled to the capital, prayerfully for the last time. Our adoptive parents were there with us in Kinshasa. We checked into a hotel for the week. While they finished up paperwork with the embassies, we spent time with family members for what seemed to be the last time. During the same week, our adoptive mom was tasked to go to Lumbubashi to retrieve Suzanne as she was also adopted and scheduled to go with us. Unfortunately, or maybe fortunately, Suzanne had other plans. On the day she was to depart with our adoptive mom, she ran away. Suzanne and I have had many conversations concerning her courageous boldness at 15 years old to walk away from the opportunity to come to the U.S. with us. Though it seemed selfish through my lenses, knowing what I know now, I have no rocks to throw at her for making the decision not to come. Of course, her unwillingness to come led to an uproar in the family. Our adoptive mom has recounted the story more times than I wish to acknowledge. She was furious, angry, and felt disrespected by Suzanne's choice. She explains that the plane ride there and back was full of turbulence, and she could have lost her life attempting to get Suzanne from Lubumbashi. She could not believe Suzanne would be so selfish and neglectful to recognize the sacrifices that she and her husband had made on our behalf. But over time all her words of frustration became just that, redundant words. And in their redundancy, her anger towards Suzanne became bitterness. She had nothing positive to say about her and this became the norm.

With Suzanne choosing not to come, the show still had to go on. Within two weeks of our arrival in Kinshasa, we headed to Cameroon where we were scheduled to pick up visas. Cameroon was intended to be a quick stop, and to save money, Naomi, my abuser, and I shared a room. Of course, in the middle of the night, my abuser found his way to my bed, woke me up and gave me directives on my sexual duties for the night. I had become numb to it all and secretly, I couldn't wait to arrive in the land of the free. As life would have it, our adoptive parents experienced some bumps in the road concerning paperwork. The American government could not comprehend how

Naomi and my abuser were both born in the Congo, while I had some documentation stating I was born in Ivory Coast. This created a delay in the issuing of my visa. My adoptive dad decided that it would be best for his wife, my abuser and Naomi to head on to the United States. He also decided that it was imperative he return to the Congo, while I stayed in Cameroon with a woman we had just recently met. Looking back, I am thankful that Psalm 68:5 promises that God is a father to the fatherless and His hand of protection was upon me even before I could fully acknowledge Him. If you have read this far, you know by now that I was thrilled to be away from my abuser, whom at the time I could only see as a despicable creature.

I spent the week with the family in Cameroon and spent most of my unencumbered time playing outdoors. Before I knew it, seven days had gone by and my adoptive dad had gotten everything that was needed for me to travel and join the rest of the family in Newport News, Virginia. On December 18, 2002, I stepped into the plane in Cameroon as an unaccompanied minor traveling to the United States. I sat at the front of the plane so the flight attendants would have access to me easily. We stopped in Paris for a few hours and oh how I wished I could have at least been able to take a picture outside of the airport. Nonetheless, I have been able to say I have stepped foot on Paris soil, and I can't wait to get an opportunity to go back for more than a transit. We landed in Dulles airport on December 19, 2002. I was told my oldest female cousin on our paternal side lived nearby in Woodbridge, Virginia, and that her husband would be picking me up. I chuckle thinking about this concept of sending someone I had never met or seen in pictures to come pick up a minor! Yet, there he was standing by the luggage claim with a sign "Njiba Kasonga." While I couldn't speak English, I at least could read and recognize my own name. The flight attendant passed the baton of oversight to my cousin's husband and there began my journey of many unknowns in the land of the free.

I can't assume that everyone knows exactly what it is like to be surrounded by people whose language you can't understand. What I can however predict is that many people have at least experienced being in unfamiliar places, meeting new people or doing something for the first time. After hearing, reading, talking and thinking about America, I had finally arrived. Many people around me spoke English, and I did not know one single word. Within the first few minutes of leaving the airport, I knew I was no longer in the Congo. The roads were paved. There were cars everywhere and tall buildings. I saw traffic lights for the first-time directing traffic, and I was amazed by the orderly conduct of people on the interstate. As someone who can now drive, I know for a fact that the interstate is full of people who drive with no agenda of decency. But that's neither here nor there. The United States looked exactly like what they portrayed it to be in the Congo, a country with endless possibilities. It took me many years to realize that wealth and poverty are no respecter of continents. Just like there are poor people in Africa, there are poor people in America. Furthermore, the opposite is also true. In my "fresh off the boat" state however, America had no issues, and I was thrilled to be here. After spending a week in Woodbridge, Virginia, I was transported to Newport News, Virginia. It never dawned on me how vast the United State was or that it was a country made up of many states. Regardless of where I was, once again, I knew I could check off the box and claim to have landed on U.S. soil.

Being that I arrived near Christmas time, students were on break and there were many festivities happening. Not only was I meeting my cousins, who were now my siblings through adoption, but we were also on tour to meet everyone who was anticipating our arrival. My first Sunday in the country, my adoptive family and I attended Hidenwood Presbyterian Church, which eventually became a major part of my adolescence. We were greeted by many smiling faces. I had never seen so many Caucasian faces in my life. I had been in the presence of the Caucasians who came to Congo for mission work occasionally and had interacted with them with simple waves. But now, this would be my reality. I remember everyone in the church embracing us and asking questions. In those instances, I wished I had paid more attention during the few English lessons we had at Mamu

Lumingu. Unfortunately, it was too late. Therefore, the basis of our interaction was reduced to the common human expression of pleasantry, smiles. The smiles carried me through many introductions, school tours, hospital visits and many failed attempts to assimilate.

The year 2003 rolled in quickly and it was soon time to start school. I was in 7th grade and was scheduled to attend Dozier Middle School because it was the designated school for students learning English. I was informed during my tour that there was a girl who was from Africa who spoke French. As the first day of school came, my nerves quickly dissipated as I basked in the idea of having someone in my class who spoke French. But when I got on the bus, I rapidly realized that the girl I had placed my hope in was from Sudan and spoke Arabic. Talk about shaking my head! This was my first realization that Americans must not know that Africa is made of countries who often don't share the same language. But I had to quickly get over the misleading information I was given and find a way to communicate with my ESL teacher, Mrs. Guthmiller. She was a tall Caucasian woman with short hair and an enthusiastic spirit. She had a desk with my name on it. She welcomed me using the best French word she knew, BONJOUR! I was touched by her attempt to make me feel at ease. I looked around and every object in the classroom was labeled. There were pictures with words next to them on the walls. I could tell she had tried to make the classroom as comfortable as possible for her students, who were all there with one goal, to learn English. In a class with at least fifteen students, there was no other foreign student who spoke French. The Spanish speakers had a crew. The Cambodian speakers had a crew. The Arabic speakers had a crew. And then there was me. I knew right then and there that I had no time to waste. If feeling like an outsider was not motivating enough to learn English, two weeks after the start of school, pain wheezed itself through the halls of my middle school, into my math class and reminded me that though I had crossed the Atlantic Ocean, our encounter was more than a casual acquaintance. We were destined to find each other and be in a relationship.

Although I had mastered smiling my way through each day and most awkward moments at school, I found myself stuck between having a repeat of my humiliating kindergarten experience versus opening my mouth to make my needs known. There was a girl who often walked me to class who I thought was genuinely interested in being my friend. I later found out she was asked to be my school buddy and had no interest in me. Being that the math curriculum in the Congo was ahead of the one in Virginia, I was able to keep up with most of the arithmetic if they weren't in word form. Within a short period, many of the students in the class concluded that I was good at math. My school buddy casually cheated off me and I saw no issue with it because I was not able to tell the teacher or even express to her how wrong she was. Nonetheless, I figured it was a win-win situation. She helped me navigate through the school, even if it meant students laughing at me and making monkey noise as I walked past them. I on the other hand helped her in math class. It's amazing how you cannot speak the same language, yet you can communicate with someone else unknowingly. Most days while at school, I avoided the bathroom. My adoptive mom and siblings gave me the impression that the bathrooms were dirty. I therefore took it upon myself to hold any restroom needs until I got home. I can't believe I was already practicing for what my life would be like as a teacher! Nonetheless, on one specific day, I just absolutely could not hold it. I needed to go to the bathroom immediately. Because I was not in my ESL class, there was no word wall anywhere for me to undertake the task of formulating the sentence, "May I go to the bathroom?" So, I did what most twelve-year-old would do, ask a friend. Well, I asked my school buddy, who I thought was my friend. Being that I couldn't speak English, I simply tapped her and did the universal pee-pee dance. My school buddy looked at me, pointed to the teacher and without hesitation said, "F * YOU!" and no it wasn't FORGET YOU. Assuming she had just given me the key that would unlock my ability to ask the teacher if I could relieve myself, I walked to the front of the class while squeezing my legs.

"F* YOU!" I exclaimed.

The teacher looked at me with a puzzled look as the entire class burst into laughter. It's hard to know exactly what the teacher said to me in that moment. I however remember thinking to myself, maybe my accent is terrible. Maybe she doesn't understand what I am trying to tell her. So, I stood there with my legs crossed hoping I didn't pee in front of everyone and loudly exclaimed three times, "F* YOU!" And as the laughter in the class grew, it finally dawned on the teacher that one of the students more than likely was at the root of this. She immediately lightened up and asked another student to walk me to the bathroom. While I was glad to have relieved myself, a sense of shame overwhelmed me. I went home that day in tears. I was ready not to come back to school.

"What's wrong with you?" one of my adoptive siblings asked.

"I don't like it here! I asked to go to the bathroom today and everyone laughed at me," I responded angrily.

"So exactly how did you ask to go to the bathroom?" she questioned me.

"I just told the teacher F* YOU!" I proclaimed proudly.

Her eyes popped open as if I had just committed a crime. Then she proceeded to explain to me that I had used profanity towards the teacher. I simply could not believe that my school buddy would deceive me like that. I replayed the students laughing at me and it stung. I made up my mind that night that I was going to do everything in my power to learn the English language and one of those kids would pay. I didn't know how I would get them back. Yet I realized that most of them cheated off me anyways. What better way to experience revenge than by putting wrong answers on my paper, letting them copy and then asking for more time to complete mine accurately. I was told that in America you couldn't fight at school because you could get suspended. Despite my strong desire to beat my school buddy up, watching her get an F while I got an A gave me a great wicked satisfaction.

As the year went by, I slowly assimilated to the culture of the United States. I quickly realized that children did not obey their teachers and spoke to them in any way they pleased. This was shocking to me. But I suppose having corporal punishment back in the Congo potentially made our school experience different. Furthermore, we paid for school, and *when you invest in something financially, you cherish it.* Additionally, the food, clothing, entertainment, and architecture were all completely different. I wasn't sure whether I liked the change, and at the same time I had no choice but to accept the change. Change can be difficult, especially when it's something you have never encountered before. For me, experiencing winter was the biggest change of all, and after fifteen plus years in the United States, I have yet to find a love for winter. Yet I can recall the very first time the weather forecast announced that we would be getting snow. I was so excited to finally see this magical white stuff falling from the sky. We went to sleep like any other night and woke up with the ground covered with white fluff. Our adoptive family seemed to not be amazed by the snow as this had become commonplace to them. They did however advise us to wear our winter coats, gloves, hats, scarves, and boots.

I was thrilled to finally touch this unknown element I had heard and read about for many years. As I took one step outdoors, a cold wind met me, and chills went through my spine. How can these people like winter? I was skeptical without even getting to where the snow was. I slowly made my way to the grassy area and made a ball of snow. I couldn't help but wonder what it tasted like, and my curiosity won. But to my biggest disappointment, snow tasted like cold ice water. I was bummed. I expected something different. I expected something that would exceed my expectation and become a topic of discussion for the rest of my life. Instead, I was faced with the taste of what I already knew. Not to mention, I was so eager for the snow that I took off my gloves to properly feel the texture of snow. Unimpressed, I made my way back into the house to get warm. However, no one informed me that for whatever scientific reason, when you change environments, extreme cold to hot, it is possible for you to feel a painful burning sensation in your hands. Ouch! I sat by the heater in pain, hoping and wishing this feeling would go away. It eventually did. Nonetheless, I became very skeptical about calling the United States home. I wasn't sure if I would ever embrace the cold season, which occurs once a year. In my twelve-year-old mind, this moment in the U.S. held a profound lesson. Though I changed continents and countries, the pain within me was still present. Crossing the Atlantic Ocean did not change the fact that my parents were dead. Leaving Congo behind did not alter the reality that my abuser was still living in the same house as I was. Consequently, for me, the cold outside and the warm inside was an accurate depiction of my emotional state. Internally, I was angry at God, the world, and everything else I could name. Yet on the outside, I portrayed a smile of innocence as white as the snow I saw that January of 2003. Sadly, pain and I had many prior encounters, and I knew it wouldn't be long before I would experience an emotional breakdown.

Peeling the Onion

I befriended a girl in middle school who was nice to me, but she ended up moving to New York. I was sad because I felt as though I had just gained a friend. While I enjoyed the classmates I had in my ELL (English-Language Learner) class, we were all foreigners and could only relate from that standpoint. It was important for me to make friends outside of the confines of the ELL class, especially African Americans. Back then I didn't understand why African Americans were very mean to me. I was called everything from monkey, African booty scratcher to dirty and poor. It puzzled me that people who had the exact same skin color as I did were the ones I couldn't stand. Here I thought blacks were supposed to stick together. At the age of twelve I had to comprehend the underlying bitterness many African Americans held towards Africans for selling them into slavery. Many of the African Americans I encountered later confessed that they were taught to despise anything that smelled or breathed African. But Anisah was different. Whether she genuinely became my friend or not, I was completely sad when she moved. Thankfully before the age of social media, Anisah and I exchanged home addresses.

It was 2003 and hurricane Isabel had made her way to the Hampton Roads area. Like many other families, we were affected drastically by it. As we napped in our dining room, there was a loud BOOM. Due to the strong winds, a tree in the neighbor's yard behind us fell and split the top portion of the house into two unequal parts. Though we were devastated at the damage, we were grateful no one was hurt. Naomi and I were sent to stay with some good friends, the Barnes, while the rest of the adults attempted to figure out what was next. Later, as things settled with the insurance company, our family was placed in a hotel for two weeks and then an apartment for six months. It was during our time at the apartment that Anisah's letter came. In her letter she updated me on her life and proceeded to ask if I still had a crush on a boy from our school. Unbeknownst to me, my adoptive parents opened the letter prior to my arrival.

"Laura, who is this girl who wrote to you?" was the beginning of the interrogation. Laura is my middle name. In our culture, first names are reserved for school, business, and formal contexts. Middle names are often use amongst family members, church, and familiar contexts.
"It's my friend from school. She moved to New York, and we exchanged addresses."
"How old is this girl?" my adoptive mom proceeded to ask.
We're like the same age I thought to myself. "She is 14."
"How dare you! She is too old for you. So, you are befriending people older than you and discussing liking boys. Who is Mauris? Is that your boyfriend?"
With great terror I answered, "No! He is just a boy at school."
In our culture and household children rarely ever discussed sex, romance, or anything of that nature. I had no idea where this conversation would go.
"So exactly, what do boyfriends and girlfriends do?" my adoptive dad probed.

"I don't know. Hang out. Go to the movies or the mall," I answered as best as I could. He looked at me with disgust and proceed to give me the accurate answer.

"No. They F***!" he yelled the four-letter word that I could never envision him saying. I gasped for air! There was that F word again, except this time it was coming out of the mouth of a man who would have never allowed me to use profanity. I couldn't believe it. I was shocked. I didn't know whether to laugh, cry or be petrified. His definition followed many other strong words and a few slaps in the face. I felt humiliated and angry. I just wanted to be a normal girl who had friends. I wanted to be like the other kids at school who communicated with their parents. But I couldn't. I was left to face the music alone and according to my adoptive dad's definition of having a boyfriend, I had had a boyfriend since I was nine. Here they were so worried about a boy at school whom I no longer had a crush on, yet they couldn't discern that an F word was happening right underneath their nose: FORNICATION.

That night I cried myself to sleep wishing I could be normal, but given my encounters with pain, pain was the norm. I couldn't shake the idea that my abuser was my boyfriend, according to my adoptive dad's definition. I never pictured him as such but in a twisted way, I allowed myself to believe the lie. I wanted to scream and tell them I wish Mauris was my actual boyfriend. But no, instead I was stuck with this guy they willingly called their son. Essentially what I got from that interaction was that sex is bad and it is reserved for people in romantic relationships. This was the first and only conversation, or should I say monologue, I was given about sex. For people who called themselves Christians, I was taken aback that not once I was taken to Scripture to be taught what sex was intended for and how God had designed for it to be between a man and a woman in the context of marriage. I was not affirmed nor explained that having a crush as a teenager was part of the process of puberty. Unfortunately, like too many parents in the African community I witnessed, sexual education was not high on the priority list. Looking back on this incident as a parent, I truly believe this could have been an opportunity for them to both pour into my life. And as much as I am disappointed that it didn't occur, I am also aware that their parents probably never provided them with such intimate conversation. Therefore, their parenting tactics could only reflect what had been ingrained in them. *It takes boldness and courage to assess one's culture, methods or habits, and choose to critique them for what they're worth and be in a position to accept going against the stream.*

Eighth grade year came and went. By the time I was starting ninth grade, I was no longer classified as an ELL student. On paper, I had checked all the marks for knowing enough English to function academically. This did not equate however to how confident I felt about communicating in the English language. Nonetheless, I was thrilled to be out of the program because it meant I could attend the high school I was actually zoned for, Menchville High school. We had moved literally down the street from the high school, and I was excited I would not have to take the bus. As I walked into the school, there was a sign welcoming the class of 2008! It's only 2004, I reminded myself. How could they possibly be excited for 2008 already? As an educator now, I am ashamed of how many times I have spoken to students about how quickly their graduation date comes. Of course, they all look at me with the same puzzled look I had when I first walked into Menchville. Though it wasn't my first time going to school in America, I was nervous to have to be the new kid again. Most of the students who had attended Dozier Middle with me were going to the other high schools in the area. As I attempted to find my way around the building. I heard a familiar voice. Because disappointment was often waiting for me around the corner, I did not want to get my hopes up. The voice sounded like Mr. Joe Edwards, also known as Mr. E.

Mr. E. was the assistant principal at Dozier when I arrived in 7th grade. Unbeknownst to me of how the school system works, he then left Dozier. I remember hearing the news about his soon to be departure and I cried. Mr. E. never had a conversation with me that lasted more than minute. He was however, the first African American man in the United State who made me feel welcome. I could not speak English, but there was something magical about his smile. He seemed to know every student by name and talked to everyone in a jovial manner. Though he was taller, his smile reminded me of Papa's. There was warmth about his presence. Despite not being able to fully communicate with him, his absence made me despondent. It was evident that my countenance changed as soon as I looked through the glass windows of the main office and saw Mr. E.

"Njiba! It's so good to see you here!" Mr. E. exclaimed when we made eye contact.

In shock I uttered, "Mr. E., you just left. I came to school one day and you were gone."

With a proud look on his face, he placed his hand on my shoulder and said, "Wow! You speak English now. I am so proud of you Njiba. I did not leave abruptly. I was transferred to Menchville when I left Dozier."

"God must have known I would be coming here and sent you ahead so that I would know I had someone to look out for me," I responded.

"You got that right! It's going to be a great year Njiba. Please let me know if you need anything."

This was the beginning of a relationship that I am forever grateful for. My interaction with Mr. E. brought ease to my heart and somehow, I believed it when he said it would a great year. I allowed myself to be happy that day, yet in the back of my mind I was hesitant to fully commit to this happiness mostly because I felt dirty on the inside. By day I was a student and by night I was the object of a relative's sexual desire. I was suffocating in my thoughts, fears, and anger that happiness was a fleeting moment, always. I was tired of this cycle, but I did not know how I would ever get out of it.

As the day went, I met my teachers and many of them were curious about the meaning of my name and how I came to be in the U.S. I spared everyone my sob story because I was told by my adoptive parents, "What happens in our house stays in our house," which caused me to tell everyone the alternate version of the truth. My alternate version of the truth was that I came from a family of eleven children. Our father came to the United States with the first batch of my siblings and once he was stable financially, he returned for Naomi and me. Of course, no one knew me at Menchville and my story sounded reasonable, so they believed me. There were however two teachers whom I could not seem to be able to sell that story to: my math teacher Mrs. Moore and my health teacher Coach Henderson.

Mrs. Moore was an older African American woman who immediately felt like a mother to everyone in the class. She genuinely cared about her students, and she had a relationship with Jesus Christ. There were many days I would stay after school with her my 9th grade year simply to avoid going home when no one else would be there but my abuser. Mrs. Moore would take time to elaborate on anything I didn't understand in class, and I would help with anything she needed in the classroom. Through our many interactions, she would share many life nuggets with me and made me wonder if this is how things would have been had Maman still been alive. Furthermore, due to her experience and discernment, she could always tell when something was bothering me. I never fully told her the reality of what took place in my home, but she at least knew my biological parents were dead and I missed them terribly. Mrs. Moore took time to get to know me as more than a student on her roster. She encouraged me, she affirmed me, she prayed for me and for the first time in years, I felt the nurture of a mother.

Unlike Mrs. Moore, Coach Henderson took a humorous approach. As I sat in his class with twenty plus students, I struggled to see the board. When I spoke to him about it, he suggested I move up near his desk. While being near his desk, he would ask questions about my country of origin and proceed to make fun of me with the most stereotypical comments. He later introduced me to a girl from Guyana, and I introduced him to a girl from Cuba. The three of us decided to form an international group and congregate in Coach Henderson's office for lunch while he worked on his athletic director duties. None of us had many friends, so lunch in Coach Henderson's office was perfect. Over a period, the two other girls' attendance at lunch bunch decreased and I would take this opportunity to help Coach Henderson with small tasks. As we worked together, he would ask me about running through the jungles or riding my elephant to school. I would roll my eyes and attempt to educate him about my life in Congo. It was through my eager desire to prove him wrong that I was able to share with him how and why I got to come to the United States. Having a daughter himself and being a man who feared the Lord, Coach Henderson would remind me that the trials of life would pass. He encouraged me to keep my eyes on the goals I had and that one day I would see the fruits of my labor. I am so grateful to have had two teachers who despite my lack of proficiency in the English language took their time outside of class to pour into me.

While in health class, the topic of sexual reproduction came up. We were taught the biological facts of intercourse and its repercussion. I think I was probably one of the few students in the class who was amazed at all this information I had never been privileged to learn. Immediately a great fear came upon me. My abuser was also my cousin. We were having unprotected sex and I had recently had my menstrual. The idea that I could now get pregnant by him was horrid to even think about. I left health class that day wondering how I could put an end to what was happening. As I walked home from school, though I was not the praying type, I found myself talking to God. Isn't it amazing how we don't entertain the idea of God until we find ourselves in a pit? In my underdeveloped prayer life, I asked God to give me the boldness and courage to share the truth. Would they believe me, or would I be punished once again? I honestly did not know how this news would be received. What I was more afraid of however was becoming pregnant because of rape through an incestuous relationship. My heart was beating faster than it had ever had. But I had made up my mind that today was the day.

I walked into the house and found one of my adoptive siblings in the kitchen sitting at the island. She was the youngest daughter of my adoptive dad and somewhat closer to me in age. I felt comfortable sharing with her. I sat next to her and took the questioning approach.

"Is it true that if a girl has sex after she has had her period, she can get pregnant?" I asked.

She laughed and looked at me with a puzzled look. "Yes! Why do you ask?"

"Well, today in Health class we learned about intercourse and reproduction and stuff like that."

I wasn't sure how I would go from talking about a lesson in Health class to telling her that my so-called brother had been forcing me to have sex with him for the last three years and now I was panicking because I did not want to have a baby with him. I took a deep breath.

"So, you know I just had my period and I just feel like..." I spoke with hesitation.

"Laura! What are you trying to say?" she questioned me immediately.

Without thinking twice, I exhaled and said, "My abuser has been forcing me to have sex with him for the last three years. It all started when we were in Congo after Maman and Papa died. I tried telling his parents about it, but no one believed me. It's been happening here too while everyone is away. He tells me to come to his room at night. He wakes me up in the middle of the night to come. He tells me if I don't come, he will punish me the next day. He has slapped me and made me kneel for hours on the rug with spikes. He threatens to hurt Naomi because he knows I want to protect her, and he made me promise never to tell anyone."

My adoptive sister stood there in shock at what I had just told her. I couldn't believe I was bringing to light what had been in the dark for so long. I had envisioned this day for so long and when it arrived, I couldn't quite recognize what had just happened. With full confidence, my adoptive sister looked at me and said, "This ends today!" She picked up the phone, called her parents and the rest of her siblings for a family meeting. My abuser had not come home from school yet and he had no clue that his world was about to shift. When he arrived home, my adoptive parents interrogated him, and he admitted to everything I had disclosed. As soon as he acknowledged that I was not lying, there was a paradigm shift. I couldn't believe that not only were my claims taken seriously this time, but something was about to be done. My oldest adoptive sister contacted her father and told him that my abuser needed to be sent back to Africa immediately.

For the next two to three days, no one really spoke to each other. There was a perplexing atmosphere in the house. On one hand, my adoptive mom stared me down with looks of disgust and on the other hand, my adoptive dad kept asking me how I could do this to him. I was dumbfounded. How did I do this to you? I wasn't the one going to his room begging him to have sex with me. How is it my fault? Before I could compose myself, my adoptive dad asked that both my abuser and I write down what had been happening. I honestly did not have the words to recount again and again when and how it all started but I had no choice. I wrote my essay with tears in my eyes. I just wanted it all to be over. Those seventy-two hours felt like the longest days in the universe of days. My abuser's fate had been decided. His ticket had been bought and he would be returned to his biological parents in the Congo. It's hard to know what was going through his mind because we barely made eye contact. He was only 17 years old and for the first time since he chose to take my virginity away, he looked powerless. His departure day arrived. We all stood in the garage listening to my adoptive dad address him and pray for his travel. In a blink of an eye, he was gone. He didn't apologize to me. He didn't tell me why I became his target. Secretly, I was so thrilled he was gone. Yet I didn't realize that his absence what just the beginning of a journey of turmoil and distress that would have me wishing I was never born.

Purple and Gold

The first few months after my abuser left were horrible. I thought that bringing what happened to light would lighten the load that I carried internally for years, but it didn't. Instead of being supported into counseling, therapy or even discipleship, I endured many days and nights of verbal and emotional abuse. Although my adoptive dad kept repeating that he was not a man who dwells in the mud, the fornication news traveled through the airways and landed in the ears of many people in the Congolese community. My adoptive parents would pretend to want to understand my side, not asking questions about what happened but rather by accusing me of enjoying the sex so much that I chose to not tell anyone. I was called anything from whore, slut, promiscuous, wicked and Satan in human flesh. My adoptive mom was very clear about how I had brought sin into her home and that I would amount to nothing because of it. My spirit was crushed, and I no longer understood what the rules of honesty were. I had heard that honesty was the best policy, but no one told me it came with a price. For me the price was constant humiliation, being shunned and stigmatized as having a lustful spirit. I stood in front of the mirror many times calling myself the names I was labeled because it became my new reality. I was dying inside, and no one cared to ask how I was doing. My adoptive mom would tell me how happy she would be when I would finally leave her house after high school. One day I did the math. I concluded that if I didn't commit suicide before then, 2008 would be my year of freedom. It was 2004 then and four years seemed manageable. Nevertheless, counting down 1,500 days felt like it would take eternity.

With no friends to have over, sports to play, or parties to attend, I had nothing but time on my hands. This meant I could dedicate myself fully to school and church activities. Purple and gold became my favorite colors because those were the Menchville High School colors. While my world at home was collapsing, I could be anything I wanted to be at school. I spent the rest of my freshman year laying low. I did not want anyone to know how broken I was behind the smile I wore daily. Everyone in the building knew me as the foreign girl who did not speak English well and had an interesting name. To be frank, this is all I could handle people knowing and because I carried an overweight load in my heart that year, pretending I was invisible was easier.

The summer after my freshman year, I spent a few weeks in Woodbridge, Virginia, where I had initially begun my journey in the United States. There aren't many parts of my time there that I don't remember, but I know that it was the beginning of a shift I wouldn't know how to embrace until a decade later. On August 14, 2005, I attended a church in Woodbridge with my cousin and her family. I am not even sure what the sermon was about that Sunday. However, as the pastor concluded the message, the choir began to sing, "I won't go back, I can't go back to the way it used to be, before your presence came and changed me." I had never heard the song, but the lyrics tugged at my heart. The pastor started to talk about a man named Jesus who was born, lived, died, and resurrected for the forgiveness of my sins. He said that Christ wanted to set me free and that the burden I was carrying was too heavy for me to bear. He exalted His name and said accepting Christ was the only way for man to be reconciled to God. Though he was not talking to me personally, it felt as though he was. I stood there torn. On one hand I knew I did not know Jesus though I had heard of Him and been around church circles. But until that Sunday, no one had ever presented the Gospel to me so clearly and concisely. On the other hand, I had a panoramic picture of all my sins flashing before me and a voice screaming in my head, "You are worthless. Your sins are too deep. No one wants you." Thankfully, John 6:44 says, "No one can come to Me unless the Father who sent Me draws him; and I will raise him up at the last day" (NKJV), and the Holy Spirit drew me to the altar. That Sunday at fourteen years old with no full understanding of what being a Christian means, I publicly confessed with my mouth the Lord Jesus and believed in my heart that God raised Him from the dead and I was saved. The entire congregation celebrated with me and for the first time in many months I genuinely smiled. I told myself I would leave everything at the foot of the cross of Christ, cast my burden unto Him because His yoke is easy, and I embraced the idea that Jesus wanted to give me rest. Yet somehow, I had forgotten that summer would soon end. Consequently, I would be returning to my Egypt.

I returned to Newport News with hopes that things would be different than when I had left. Unfortunately, I disappointed myself. I placed unrealistic expectations on others' perspectives and ability to digest what had been going on with me and my abuser. No one asked how summer vacation was nor did I sense an interest for anyone to know that I made a commitment to spend eternity with Jesus. It was the beginning of having a double life. At home I felt tormented and outside I felt accepted. This frustration opened the door for what I thought would never happen again.

As many members of my family shunned me, a male relative by marriage begin to approach me with comforting words. He approached me from a big brother perspective. He told me I was not any of those labels people were telling me I was. He reminded me to stay focused on school and that I would make a life for myself. He told me I was intelligent and beautiful. I couldn't believe someone was affirming me. The fourteen-year-old Njiba had experienced many traumatic episodes that were not handled properly, and I had nothing to stand on. Therefore, I fell for his compliments. At first the compliments seemed genuine. I was a young lady who looked at his outward appearance without any wisdom or discernment to know the motive of his heart. He gave me his number and asked that I would call him anytime I just needed to talk or if I needed anything. I took him at his word. In the weirdest way, we became friends, and it was as though my heart became fond of him. It didn't matter how I was mistreated by others. I knew I had a big brother who had my back.

Then one day as he was over at the house, we sat in the family room talking about school and life like we typically would, but something was different. That day my big brother and friend became my violator. He began to look at me with desiring eyes and lusting after me. He told me I was beautiful and that my breasts were perky just the way he likes them. He came near me, fondled them, and smiled. I stood there in shock because I had been to this movie before and knew it would not end well. Yet for some reason I felt paralyzed. How was it that he could deem what my abuser had done as sinful and now choose to violate my trust? I suspect he sensed the confusion within me. He hugged me and said, "Don't worry. No one must find out. Don't tell anyone!" and like a programed robot, I forced a smile and said, "sure."

I was disgusted with myself. I couldn't believe I had told Jesus I was tired of living a lie and here I was picking up again what I supposedly left at the cross. I knew I needed to tell someone because my violator came around the house often and we would go to their house as well. I knew he and I would have more encounters alone. I knew that he wouldn't stop at fondling my breast once. Though he was in his thirties, and I was fourteen, my expectations for him to make wiser decisions seemed out of the question. In my underdeveloped brain, I couldn't fathom going to my adoptive parents or siblings with this news. What would I say? Well, I know it took me two years to tell you about my abuser and I told myself I would never wait again. So here is another truth, I now have a violator. I knew I would be crucified. So, I stayed silent. My violator took my silence as a sign of approval. Fondling turned into kissing. Kissing turned into oral sex. Oral sex turned into intercourse. Not once. Not twice, but multiple times. Every time I lay in bed with him, I asked myself repeatedly why I was doing this. I would remember my altar call experience and knew Jesus died to set me free, yet I was in bondage to sexual perversion. With me knowing how to live a double life, I kept my little secret to myself my entire sophomore year, smiling outwardly and bleeding internally.

And then it happened. One month I missed my menstrual cycle and the thought of being pregnant at fifteen with, yet another family member's child petrified me. I did what most girls do when they think they are pregnant and contacted my violator via email. In my email I expressed that I no longer wanted to live tormented with the fear of getting caught, being pregnant or being the promiscuous person, I was labeled to be. My violator casually dismissed my email, and I was left to wait for "Aunt Flo," praying she made her monthly appearance. I went about my day casually without knowing that I never signed out of my email account from the family computer. That afternoon, my adoptive father did his habitual routine when he got home and sat at the computer. Until this day, I have no idea how it all happened. Before I could gather my thoughts, my adoptive dad had printed my email exchange with my violator and was interrogating me about our relationship. I had no choice but to choose truth once again. I knew it would be costly. I knew I would be crucified. But I also somehow knew that walking in truth meant walking in freedom. Proverbs 28:13 states, "He who covers his sins will not prosper, but whoever confesses and forsakes *them* will have mercy" (NKJV), and while I had no knowledge of this verse at the time, I knew I wanted to prosper.

By the next day, my violator and his wife were at the house for a family meeting. At this point, my adoptive mom did not even want to share the same oxygen with me, let alone the same space. My violator's wife looked as if she had been crying during their entire ride to the house. She was angry and greeted with me, "You are a whore, Laura! You are a true b****. You are going to hell." All I could think of was that she was probably right. I deserved this anger, but shouldn't she have been mad at her husband? That wasn't for me to decide though. My adoptive dad called the meeting to start by asking me all the questions he had already asked me prior to their arrival. I answered every question truthfully while staring at my violator. Then to be fair, my adoptive dad asked my violator what he had to say about the claims I was making and the email evidence. My violator looked straight at me almost as if to have a staring contest and said, "Papa, how could you believe her? Laura is delusional. How can you believe someone who we just found out was having sex with her abuser and didn't say anything? Everything she is saying is a lie. I have never slept with her, nor have I been in contact with her. She is delusional. I don't know if she is going through puberty and fantasizing about having sex with me, but this is a lie."

I think I stopped breathing for a few seconds because I was in total shock. I couldn't believe this man whose penis had entered the most sacred part of my human anatomy could look me in the eyes and call me delusional. While this was hurtful, what was more painful was that everyone else believed him. His wife and my adoptive mom began to insult me with every negative word they could think of. They swung at me with wooden spoons or anything they could reach. Next thing I knew I was pinned up against the fridge getting beaten up and insulted at the same time. Unexpectedly, one of my adoptive siblings picked me up and ran me upstairs to my room. He instructed me not to leave the room unless he was around. I will forever be grateful for him providing that escape and if you ever land eyes on this book, thank you.

And so it was, once again I was the demonic force in the house according to my adoptive parents. With two sexual scandals, my adoptive mom was convinced that I practiced witchcraft and I was sent to destroy her household. At the time I didn't know the level of dysfunction in their lives, but because everything got blamed on me, I accepted that everything was my fault. I was once again treated with the silent treatment. The difference this time was that because this happened with a relative that was rather close to my adoptive parents, the scandalous news did not travel as quickly or as far as it did with my abuser. Yet like my abuser, my violator and his family decided to be secluded from us. They no longer came to the house, nor did I go to theirs. I spent many nights having nightmares of a man coming into my room ready to force me into intercourse. In my nightmare I would scream and attempt to fight him off. He always won. I was powerless while I was awake, and I was powerless while I slept. Again, no counseling, therapy, discipleship or intervention took place. I didn't have anyone to share my emotions or thoughts with. Consequently, like many other times, I existed rather than lived.

If you thought I had no life before as a teenager, two scandals meant my opportunities to be a regular high school student were out of the question. I did not attend any dances, any games, school trips or anything my adoptive parents deemed fun. I spent many days staring at our backyard and pretending I was somewhere else. I could not wait to graduate and leave the nest. Many nights I really wished I had never been adopted by anyone and that I was just left in the Congo to fend for myself like other orphans. The United States was supposed to be my happily ever after, but it felt more like hell with a piece of heaven called Menchville High. School was the only place I felt I could thrive. As a teacher now, I never underestimate the baggage that my students carry, and I aim to be a source of positivity for my students because it was done for me.

By junior year, it was the academic year 2006–2007 and I was getting close to my exit year. I was finally a proficient English speaker and had become active in the school. I made sure I signed up for anything that would keep me out of the house. I became part of the News Anchor team, which meant I needed to arrive at school early. I started working with an after-school program called 21st Century run by Newport News Public Schools for third through fifth graders, which meant I would get home at 6 PM if I wasn't scheduled to work at Dairy Queen from 6:30 PM–11:30 PM. I was fifteen years old managing multiple schedules. I stayed busy to avoid my reality. People on the outside would praise me for the works of my hands and people internally tarnished my character. At the same time, I was angry. I was angry at myself, angry at the world and angry at God. Where was He during all this? Did He even care? Sunday after Sunday I sang songs which proclaimed my adoration and love for Him, yet the posture of my heart did not mirror what my mouth confessed. Nevertheless, not going to church was not an option.

With my adoptive dad working with the Presbytery of Eastern Virginia, we visited many churches throughout the year but were always members of Hidenwood Presbyterian Church. The church had gone through a few pastoral transitions since we had first arrived in

2002 and with many of the congregation being elderly, the board was intentional about hiring young people to lead the youth. In 2006, I received a personal invitation to join the youth group lead by Lindsay Conrad. I did not know who Lindsay was, but she had a group of friends from Christopher Newport University who were apparently passionate about Jesus, the youth and ready to take the world by storm. Our first meeting did not have many people, but Lindsay became invested in all of us immediately. She would call us, text, email or meet up with us if we needed to talk. She developed lessons that were engaging and challenged us spiritually. As the few of us gathered and became comfortable with each other, we started inviting others to this amazing youth group we were attending. Eventually we no longer wanted to be just Hidenwood's youth group and decided as a group that we would be known as Alpha Omega (AO). Quite frankly, I did not know this name of God, but I have since learned to embrace Him as my beginning and my end.

As a group, we participated in fundraising events, attended retreats, and did many unplanned things together. Outside of the Menchville walls, AO became my other family. It's through the loving and safe atmosphere at AO that I slightly began to open about things that had happened to me. I wasn't bluntly parading my past or present with everyone, but I felt safe with Lindsay, our leader. We became such a huge part of Lindsay's life that she introduced us to her biological family. Lindsay's mom, Mama Conrad as I like to call her, embraced each one of the AO members and has stayed connected to me even now that I am married. I always enjoyed watching the Conrads interact as a family. Secretly, I was a bit jealous that I didn't have what they had as a family: unity, stability, friendship, honesty, and love. Yet with every encounter I had with Mama Conrad, her loving touch gave me hope. She reminded me that healthy families can exist and one day, I wanted to be intentional about creating my own.

One of the traditions at Hidenwood Presbyterian and many churches is this idea of having a youth Sunday. This is a Sunday where the youth shines and pretty much takes over the service. For the AO crew, this was an exciting day. Lindsay had worked diligently with the adults of the church to give the youth the opportunity to have total control of the service and not just some parts. Consequently, even the sermon had to be delivered by the youth group. Customarily, the high school seniors were responsible for the sermon. This seemed to be their last hoorah and moment of glam before leaving for college. Well, I happened to be a senior that year and Lindsay asked me to prepare my sermon. Though I was nervous, this was a familiar place for me. While in the Congo at the age of six, our church had a similar program, and I was selected to do the sermon. Unlike this time, at six I was simply tasked to read the message our youth pastor had written and deliver it with power. I can still envision myself on the pulpit at such a young age and thinking to myself after all the accolades from the parents that preaching may become my thing. That thought was fleeting with time, but somehow, here I was being chosen again for such a time as this.

I carefully prepared my sermon and unfortunately, I cannot recall one word I uttered on that youth Sunday. I had to run the sermon by Lindsay, and we have both tried to dig up that sermon unsuccessfully. What is true however, is that preaching that sermon caused a shift in the trajectory of my life. After much applause from the congregation and multiple praises from certain adults, many members were curious about what lay ahead for me upon graduating high school. It was May of 2008 and many universities had already decided their upcoming freshman class and all application deadlines were closed. With each question, I smiled and said I did not know where I would end up. A few people even asked me if I was considering seminary school. I knew for a fact that unless God parted the sky and told me to go to seminary school, this was not an option. I was sure I would be heading to medical school to become a doctor and in my seventeen-year-old mind, my will be done. Yet unlike all the other adults asking questions, there was an elderly couple whom I had seen in the church but never really spoken to who reassured me that God would take care of me.

Dr. Stanley and Connie Mitchel approached me on their way out of the church to ask me, like everyone else, what university I would be attending in the fall. By this time, I was tired of repeating the same thing to everyone and I sadly told them I was undecided between Old Dominion University and Virginia Commonwealth University. Dr. Stan asked why I had not made a choice and I quickly told him my reasons were financial. He looked me in the eyes with confidence and said, "Don't worry, God will take care of it." I smiled and looked at him like he had lost his mind. He then asked me if I had considered applying to Christopher Newport University. This was the dreadful question I had avoided my last two years in high school. I politely said I had not and that I was not planning to do so. Plus, all deadlines had already passed. Dr. Stan scratched his head jovially and said, "Have you met Dr. Webb? He works at CNU. Let me introduce him to you." I didn't like how this was playing out, but I followed him anyway.

CHAPTER 5: PRISON BREAK

Enough

Not every child in America gets the opportunity to attend college. Many parents envision their kids going to college one day as means to a better income and lifestyle. These parents tend to have college talks with their kids and help guide them into making the best choice based on their options. On the other hand, some parents can't possibly see it happening due to their financial situation or higher education not being the norm in the family. I had neither. Most of Papa's siblings were educated and well-off financially. This made education a priority to them and shining academically equated to one's brightness in life. Yet by the same token, my adoptive parents made it clear that they couldn't afford sending me to school. Though saddened by the news I had received, I was determined to go to college as far away from Newport News as possible. My ideal choices were any universities in California. This ensured that I would be removed from the agonizing environment I was currently in. Secondly, I was guaranteed that my adoptive parents would not pop in randomly to see me. In my search for colleges, I quickly learned that there was such a thing as in-state and out-of-state tuition. It dawned on me that it wouldn't be financially responsible to attempt going to a school outside of Virginia. I knew many universities were an option, but I was determined not to attend Christopher Newport University. This was the school three of my adoptive siblings had attended and it was fifteen minutes away from where my adoptive parents lived. There was no way I wanted this for myself. I knew that environment felt like prison and college would be my ultimate prison break.

As I applied to different schools around the state, many offered me scholarships that were enough to cover a quarter or half of my school fees. This was devastating and I had made peace with taking out loans for school. My choices came down to Old Dominion University in Norfolk and Virginia Commonwealth in Richmond.

Neither of my adoptive parents took me to college tours, so I had never seen these campuses. I was willing to go to an unfamiliar territory because my familiar was no longer a territory suitable for me. Just as I was getting excited with thoughts of freedom, my adoptive father made a point that I shouldn't take out loans. Yet when I asked what his solution was or if he would help with the remainder of the fees, his reply was always, "We don't have money." While this was aggravating, looking back I am thankful they didn't pay for my education. I have yet to cease hearing about how they spent so much money to bring me to America. And despite these efforts, according to them I am an ungrateful human being who chooses not to live my life at their beck and call.

Dr. Stan was right! God did have a plan and would take care of me. After he introduced me to Dr. Webb, I was pleasantly surprised that Dr. Webb worked as the director of the I.T. Department at Christopher Newport University. Dr. Webb encouraged me to apply to CNU despite the deadlines and to contact one of his staff members because they could offer me a job on campus. These people did not know me, yet one sermon had me in their frontal lobe. Reluctantly, I followed Dr. Webb's advice that Sunday night and applied to Christopher Newport University. Suddenly, within a few days I had received an acceptance letter with a scholarship for $1,000. During that same week, I went on campus and interviewed to work at the Information Technology Help Desk and the job was favorably mine. By the next Sunday, Dr. Stan followed up with me about my school endeavors. I told him I had gotten into CNU, but I was still short $14,500. Dr. Stan smiled and reassured me once again, "God will take care of it." I was amazed at the faith Dr. Stan had in God. I suppose after being alive for more than eighty years he had seen God work in ways I had yet seen, and he could stand on God's faithfulness.

The next day, I received a phone call from the registrar's office at CNU. The woman on the other line informed me that a check for $14,500 was dropped off at CNU that morning to pay for my expenses. My jaw quickly fell, and I had to quickly find my voice to thank her for letting me know. I was in disbelief. I knew Dr. Stan said God would take care of it, but I didn't really believe God would take care of it. The first question I asked myself was who in their right mind paid for me? After hanging up the phone I told my adoptive dad that I would be attending CNU and did not have to pay for anything. Though he rejoiced with me, he immediately started making phone calls to find out who had gifted me tuition. We later found out that Dr. Stan and Connie Mitchel decided to be the earthly vessel God used to put my heart at ease. It's hard to describe the amount of ease I felt to know that my needs had been met, and I don't believe I had done anything to deserve such grace.

My adoptive father took it upon himself to send emails to Dr. Webb and Dr. Mitchell to thank them for their assistance. It was a beautiful email of gratitude, yet his words to me afterwards were diametrically opposite of the sentiment he had virtually sent. Somehow in his mind, I was receiving this act of benevolence because of him. He proceeded to remind me about how hard it was to bring me to America and that I had put him and his wife through many trials for committing sexual sin in their home and I should have been sent back with my abuser. My heart ached as I listened because a simple "I am proud of you" would have sufficed for once. Instead, I was reminded of painful memories and how it was essentially my duty to become a doctor one day and take care of the family. If I had the power to speed time, I would have fast forwarded past his lecture into my days of freedom. I had had enough.

Captain

Prom and graduation could not come fast enough. It was the first time my adoptive parents agreed that I would at least attend prom since I barely ever did anything. I was so excited to finally do something that normal teenagers in America did. Being that I was working for Newport News Public School and Dairy Queen, I had enough money to buy my outfit. I wanted to go to the mall or at least a fancy shop, but instead I was taken to the thrift store. I found something decent there and convinced myself I would make the best of that night. As prom approached, I continued to work and prepared myself to be a CNU student. I did not know anyone else at Menchville who would be attending CNU and not many of my fellow coworkers at D.Q. aspired for college, but they were fun people to be around.

Because I went to school during the day, I often worked late shifts at Dairy Queen, getting off at 11 PM or midnight. I would often catch a ride home since my adoptive parents would be asleep by then or worst-case scenario walk home. One evening, I decided that I would simply go home later than usual. I knew my adoptive parents never waited up for me and I thought I could hang with my friends. I clocked out of work, chatted with my coworkers, and then decided to go see a friend who was a boy, aka my high school boyfriend. To be quite honest, I know he never asked me out, but we were in such frequent contact that we pretty much claimed each other. He was African and had recently come to the U.S. When we first met through his mother, he did not speak English and he was attracted to me. He expressed his sudden crush towards me to his mother and asked her if she could introduce us. His mom did introduce him to me one day; we exchanged numbers and the rest was history.

Being that he and I did not attend the same high school because he was a few years older than me and on track for Job Corps in Washington D.C., much of our interaction happened over the phone. So anytime he was in town, we tried very hard to see each other without me letting my adoptive parents know I was seeing someone romantically. That night after my shift, I thought I was safe to hangout a little longer. Unbeknownst to me, that was the exact night my adoptive dad decided to stay up and see if I had made it home on time. Around 2 AM, my phone started ringing and it was one of my adoptive siblings. My heart sunk because he and I didn't have a relationship that would warrant a 2 AM phone call. When I didn't answer he texted, "Where are you? Papa and Maman are looking for you. The police are here. I went to D.Q. twice and you aren't there. You need to come home now!" Knowing my environment, my boyfriend immediately called a taxi to get me home. Though I looked calm outwardly, I had no idea what my consequences would be when I got home. To avoid more problems than I was already in, I had the taxi drop me off closer to the house so that I could walk home and keep the identity of my boyfriend sealed.

As I approached the house, the cops were indeed at the house attempting to figure out what they should do. One of the officers started questioning my whereabouts. I told him I was hanging out with my friends after work. The officer proceeded to ask my age and I said, seventeen. The question caught me by surprise as he said, "Why didn't you just ask your parents?" My emotions were shooting bullets of anger because this man had no idea what my reality was. I looked at him and simply said, "Because the answer is always no." The police officer smiled and reminded me that I was still a minor, which meant I needed to follow the rules of my parents. I simply agreed and could not wait for the few months to pass until I left for college. As the police officers left, I could see the demeanor of my adoptive parents changing. As I walked in, my adoptive mom exclaimed, "You are no longer welcome here. Pack your belongings and when you leave in August, don't come back." Sadly, those were probably the best words she has ever uttered to me. I honestly could not wait to leave and had I been able to leave that same night, I would have left. My adoptive dad on the other hand told me I needed to write an essay concerning my whereabouts and that I could no longer go to prom.

Of course, he would take away the one thing I was looking forward to. Not only could I not go to prom, but I was also no longer allowed to work at Dairy Queen. It was two weeks before prom and a few weeks prior to graduation. I couldn't believe I would be spending the summer prior to going to college staring at the same walls I had been staring at for the last six years, and it seemed like hell had open its doors for me once again. But at this point, I knew my freshman year of college was paid for and I had already endured so much that June, July, and August would be a breeze. Prom night came and I was still within my two weeks' notice at D.Q. While my classmates celebrated, I was serving customers their food. I was too ashamed to tell anyone why I couldn't come to prom. I simply told everyone I had been scheduled to work that night, but I would come to after-prom. So, I decided to leave work early and make it to after-prom for about an hour. When I arrived, I felt like an outcast among my own classmates. Everyone was still dressed in their best outfit, and I had changed into a casual outfit. People were smiling and reminiscing on the good times they had just had. I couldn't join the conversation and I knew it was time to go.

I left the after-prom party ready for the last few days of high school to wind down. The festivities came and went. At the senior award ceremony, after all the awards were given, Mr. Surry announced that there was one award left, the principal's award. He detailed what it meant to be a recipient of this award and stated that if he could entrust the building to any student, it would be the recipient of this award. Somehow, I missed the memo that he was honoring me with this award, and then I heard students in the auditorium whisper my name. I couldn't believe that among the many students of excellence Menchville's class of 2008 had to offer, Mr. Surry would choose me. Shocked, I made my way to the stage to receive my award. Unlike many of the students there, I had no one who shared my DNA to partake in this moment with me. Though I felt sad, this was typical, and I had learned to be content with being celebrated outside my own home.

Receiving the principal's award gave me hope for the future. I somehow knew then that there was a bigger plan for my life than what I could see. I was determined after graduation to throw away most of my belongings and pack the few items I would take to college. I knew once I left what I was able to call the nest for the last six years, I wouldn't return. Though Naomi would still be living there, I had come to terms with the idea of finding other means to see her. We celebrated my graduation with family members and people from the Congolese community. When all the glam was over, I began to count the days until move-in day. I didn't have anything bought for my dorm and I was completely fine with the idea of sleeping on the floor. You know you have had enough when the thought of mediocrity in peace is more appealing than having material things without peace.

Move-in day came, and I loaded the few items I had in my adoptive dad's car. My adoptive mom went to work, and we never said goodbye. After all, this was the day we had both been waiting for, and I suppose neither one of us wanted to accurately show how thrilled we were. Nevertheless, my adoptive dad being who he is as the "family" man who attempts to keep the peace took me to the campus and Naomi came along. The car ride was mostly silent and awkward. The night before my adoptive dad attempted to have a conversation with me about boys. He expressed that there would be boys interested in me and that I was finally at the age when I could have a boyfriend. I just smiled, embarrassed at the thought that this conversation was seriously taking place. Neither adoptive parent had taken the time to cultivate emotional conversations, yet suddenly it was okay for me to have a guy interested in me. I found the whole thing hypocritical. I had no choice but to listen. I had already entertained boys without their approval and getting it now was not a relief. When he was done lecturing, I simply tested the water by asking if they would be okay if I married someone outside of the Congolese culture. My adoptive dad chuckled and ensured me that my husband must be a Muluba.

I guess the residues of that conversation lingered into the next day and made our fifteen-minute drive seem like forever. I sat there facing the front and watching the trees to distract myself. I couldn't believe my day of freedom had finally arrived. *But no one told me that being removed from prison doesn't mean you are truly free.* I knew after the cop incident that I was kicked out of their house. I knew my adoptive mom did not want my sinful and filthy self in her house. Angry at the circumstances, I vowed that day to never go back and live there. I knew there would be days of tough times, but I was willing to sleep on the street before I returned there. Upon our arrival on CNU's campus, I said my goodbyes. My adoptive dad insisted that he go and pick up a few groceries for me from a store nearby. Upon dropping off the items, his parting words were, "Remember you have a family.

Come visit us sometimes." I smiled outwardly. It pained me to hear such words. Since the death of my biological parents, I had not felt remotely close to family. I couldn't come to terms with the fact that a few months earlier as a means of punishment, they told me to never come back again. However, when the point of no return was finally here, my adoptive dad was extending an invitation I gladly declined without ever saying a word.

Free With Chains

Anyone who attends Christopher Newport University is familiar with its mascot, the Captain. Transitioning to college life was not anything I had envisioned. After I unpacked the few items, I had brought with me, a high school friend of mine Anjinai and her aunt Sharon stopped by with a freshman year care package. I had expressed to Anjinai that my adoptive parents would probably not take me shopping for my dorm and I wouldn't be able to get many things myself. Being the big-hearted person that she is, Anjinai shared my situation with Aunt Sharon, who then agreed to shop for me while she shopped for Anjinai. On move-in day, both were like angels assigned to remind me that I have a father in heaven that cares for me through the least unexpected earthly vessels.

Just like our dean had told us during our freshman welcome week, four years of undergrad went by faster than I ever wanted them to go. Being at CNU, however, allowed me to experience life in a fresh way and not always in the manner I thought it would be. I declared my major as biology with the hopes of becoming a doctor like my biological father. To keep up with my French, I chose to minor in French. While juggling my heavy science schedule, I worked at the I.T. Help Desk and for an after-school program through Newport News Public Schools. My hands were full, and I could barely handle everything that was on my plate. I was determined nonetheless to become a doctor, to have good grades, and to never have to ask my adoptive parents for anything.

At seventeen, life seemed grand, and I purposed not to visit my old stomping ground, nor did I make any phone calls. Reciprocally, my adoptive parents weren't making the effort to reach out either, so my life went on. I had a few relatives contacting me asking me to reach out and I simply said I would consider, but never did. Freshman year I lived in a suite with three girls: Natalie, Tara and Rikki. Our upbringing, experiences and aspirations were all different, yet what unified us was being on this path of discovery, together. During our first year, we bonded in many special ways. We laughed, cried, fussed, partied, and had endless conversations concerning boys. I had come to college attempting to maintain my relationship with my boyfriend from high school. I quickly realized that our paths were diverging. He did not understand my need to be engrossed in my books on the weekend or my inability to talk for hours on the phone. This tension created a friction between us that led me to utter the words all of us hate to hear, "It's not you. It's me." He did not understand my decision because he loved me dearly and professed, he would marry me. I on the other end had no words that were good enough to explain that our season was over. And if I had to be brutally honest with myself, I would say I came to realize I was trapped in making a relationship work and couldn't entertain all the eye candy Captains CNU had to offer.

Amid sorting all these emotions and attempting to maintain a high-grade point average, my roommates became my family. Natalie was the only person who had a car and she assisted me with transportation often. She invited all of us to meet her parents and visit their home. The Woltz family was very welcoming, and I am forever grateful that our paths met. During storms, breaks or just randomly, they had opened their home to us. Natalie was the youngest of two. Their family of four was richly woven by a thread, love. I thoroughly enjoyed meeting many of my friends' families. I loved the laughs we shared, the honest conversations and the joy that surrounded our outings. Yet secretly, my heart was aching. Every encounter was a reminder of what I longed to have but didn't. So instead of being a party pooper, I always chose to cherish the moments. I thanked God that even though my family dynamics weren't always the same, at least He had provided me with people who could do life with me in such a way that I didn't live with a void.

While I minded my business one day on campus, I received a call from one of my adoptive sisters letting me know that my adoptive father had a stroke and was in the hospital. I was surprised by the news, but I didn't panic. As my husband likes to say, I am the type of person who does not lose sleep over many things, nor do I respond frantically. I thanked her for the news and before I could hang up, she said, "Christmas is around the corner and with this happening, we all plan to be home." I gagged internally at the thought of calling that place home. My adoptive mom had made it clear that once I left, I shouldn't come back, and I couldn't see myself being there celebrating the holidays as if things were great. Before I could finish my thought, my phone rang again and this time it was my adoptive mother. She rarely ever called me. So, any time I saw her number come up I knew she was calling for my assistance, money, to insult me or there was a tragic family event. I answered reluctantly. There was no hello, how are you and how is school? She proceeded immediately to, "Laura, we need money to pay for papa's hospital bill. Everyone is contributing and we need $500.00 from you." I immediately rolled my eyes because I don't know what else I was expecting. Here I was a freshman in college with two part-time jobs, barely making $300.00 a month, and I was expected to somehow give $500.00. She did not let me think this through nor did it seem like I had a choice. She hung up shortly after as I stood there speechless.

I had prayed, cried, and dreamed of the day when I would be free from them. My adoptive mother's words to leave her house were my inspiration for four years of high school. I just knew leaving their physical presence would mean forever goodbye. I outwardly labeled them as my family, but internally I had accepted the idea of being done. Yet I found myself that December afternoon experiencing false freedom. I was physically free, but I still carried the chains. There was nothing obliging me to give or go to their house. However, I was afraid, and this fear of men had a grip on me. I sat there thinking how I could come up with $500.00. Not because I cared about the hospital bill but because I was afraid. I was afraid of additional rejection. I was afraid I couldn't be the hero of the day. I was afraid I would be viewed as an ungrateful person. After all, they had done "so" much to bring me to the United States. My brain's cells ran rapid with false guilt. I did not have the money, but I was determined to find a solution. When I explained to my roommates what was being asked of me, they all looked at me with a confused look and someone even asked, "Aren't they the ones who need to provide for you?" All I could do was put my head down. Of course, it would be nice as a seventeen-year-old to have parents who would support me, but this was not my reality, which in turn made me miss my biological parents even more. I didn't have time to dwell on their deaths. I had $500.00 to come up with in less than two weeks. Thankfully, Natalie offered to give me the money and I agreed to pay her back.

Christmas break came around and I was dreading spending my entire month off with my adoptive family. Since the I.T. office would be open a few days after the New Year, I asked my boss if I could come work. This meant I would only be spending two weeks with them. Interesting enough, one of my adoptive siblings who lived in Kansas would be giving birth around the same time and my adoptive mother traveled to welcome her grandkids. This made me happy because the aura of her presence was unpredictable, but often unpleasant. When I arrived at the house, the rest of the family had come, and I could tell my adoptive father was not his usual self. He questioned why I had not been coming by. I recommunicated that I was kicked out and told never to come back. He gave his classic response that he gives to many things when he is in the wrong, "who told you that? This is your home. I don't like to dwell in the mud."

It took me a long time to realize that not dwelling in the mud does not equate to accepting responsibility or asking for forgiveness. Once again, my thoughts, emotions and experiences were not acknowledged or validated. The sad part is, this had become common, and I allowed myself to be entangled in the chains of dysfunctionality. I spent my two weeks at the house with the rest of the family attempting to have the holiday cheer. I wore a mask and pretended that we were one happy family whose bond needed assistance, but these were the cards I had been dealt with and I should get with the program. I gave my $500.00, I obeyed my "parents" by coming to their beck and call and helped with taking care of my adoptive father. I checked off my good deed list with an aching heart while experiencing glimpses of hope because I had made up my mind then that my smile would never fade.

CHAPTER 6: RUINED

Long Distance

"Don't talk to strangers" can be considered the universally accepted parental code of conduct when instilling social etiquette in your children. Yet with the explosion of the digital age, it is no longer unheard of for two strangers to become friends virtually prior to meeting face-to-face. Before dating sites were accepted as a substantial format to meet your mate, online dating was a taboo. Many people did not trust the idea of communicating with a stranger, let alone trusting that people are who they say they are. Now, I am neither advocating nor bashing online dating. I know it has its pros and cons. I have seen online dating turn into beautiful marriages for some and for others, chaos waits in cyber space.

Upon exploring Myspace in high school, which I wasn't allowed to have to begin with, I found myself on a social media network called hi5. While Facebook had just begun to gain momentum in the U.S., for many Europeans and Africans, hi5 was the thing. I created a profile under one of my names, Bebela, as to avoid many people discovering my identity. I befriended and friended some people that I knew and with others, it was a game of chance. There were many Congolese people on the site. Because Hampton Roads does not have a strong Congolese or African presence, I was captivated by the ability to be connected to people who shared similar roots as me.

On a random fall day in 2008, I received a message from a guy who lived in a southern state of the U.S. He expressed that he had just come to the U.S. not too long ago and his English was not that great. He shared that he was getting to know people and wouldn't mind having me as a friend. Given my desire to help everyone, I felt compelled to undertake another saving project. Had I been emotionally mature I would have seen a pattern that resembled the last guy I had dated and recently broken up with. But they say love is blind and they are wrong. *Love walks in truth, and truth is not blinding. Lust on the other hand is blind.* My hi5 friend gave me his number and the next day, I called. Looking back, I probably seemed thirsty and craving for male attention. I didn't even play hard to get.

Our initial conversation lasted for a long time and by March 2019 I was on a flight heading to meet him. Within our very first conversation, we disagreed on a few things, and he was adamant that he was right, and I was wrong. He was older than me by about ten years and he was quick to pull the age card. I remember being taken aback by how he made me feel, *yet when you are wounded with no proper care, you settle for anything that can heal temporarily.* As time went on, we talked on the phone and skyped often. We chatted on Yahoo messenger and used every means of technology we possibly could. He never asked me to be his girlfriend, but by the nature of our conversations, I was, and I couldn't imagine my life without him. I was infatuated with the idea of him and loved him all within the same breath. There were red flags about the way we communicated, but again lust is blind. One day I voiced my concerns to him and told him he treated me as if he was my father. I told him I had a father figure and didn't need him to be that. I even went as far as telling him I felt as though I was in a dictatorship relationship. As you can imagine, his male ego and pride did not take this well. To punish me, as he later told me, he broke up with me.

I was devastated. I had experience with heart shattering moments but for some reason, this rejection hurt like never before. I found myself sick to the bone and at loss of all hope. I was so heartbroken that I found myself visiting my primary doctor, who ordered me to stay home for a week and rest. The flu had found its way into my body as if I needed another thing to cause me to see my own frailty. Yet there I was, in bed with a fever and my mind racing with a million thoughts. How could he break up with me? Is this a consequence of my sins? Would there ever be a man who would choose to marry me? None of these questions truly made sense to me, but in my desperation to feel better I allowed myself to wallow in my distress. Sadly, this is what we choose to do as humans when we have come to the end of ourselves. We search within when we aren't the ones who hold the world in our hands, even if we think we do. The part I found difficult to accept was that I had not only given him my heart, mind, and emotions. I had also given him my body, sexually. Though I really wanted to abstain from sex before marriage knowing it was dishonoring God, I chose to compromise for the sake of love and a future with him. He told me he would marry me, and I believed him. I believed him yet I did not seek counsel from those who were wiser than me nor did I seek to know what God had to say concerning our relationship. He checked many of my boxes. I liked older guys. He enjoyed traveling. He was from Congo and a Muluba. We had many things in common. It made sense on paper and in my heart. But no one told me that the heart of man was desperately wicked and outside of the Holy Spirit reigning in it, our decisions are often led by our will, intellect, and emotions.

It was Spring of 2011 and I spent much of my time away from my now ex-boyfriend immersed in other things. I traveled, I met new friends and begin to envision my life differently. During this split-rock moment, I found myself gravitating back to Abba. Out of nowhere, I found myself hungry for God in a way I had never been before. My freshman year of college I had really struggled with the idea of being a Christian. I did not know if I was truly a Christian or if I had just blindly followed religious beliefs that were set before me. Though I would acknowledge God, Jesus and occasionally attend church, my life was not bearing any biblical fruits. As God often does, His Holy Spirit drew me near when I had obviously nowhere else to turn. My romantic relationship was non-existent. My family relationships were hanging by fear. I didn't have children. This was the perfect time for the Lord to tug at my heart. Though I had taken courses to learn about other religions and intrigued my interest with other denominations, there was a void nothing seemed to fill.

One of my cousins who was in the military had introduced me to a church called Calvary Chapel Newport News (CCNN) under the leadership of Pastor Tony Clark and his wife Jenise. I had never heard of the church since I was an active participant in the Presbyterian circles while living with my adoptive parents for six years. Nonetheless, I had visited CCNN sporadically and really enjoyed the church. There was at least a thousand people who attended the church. They offered multiple service times. I was amazed at the worship and blessed to be taught chapter by chapter, verse by verse through the Bible. I knew nothing about their doctrines or theology. I knew they were a non-denominational church, diverse, who loves Christ and that was the remedy I needed. Because I only had a year left before I graduated and pursued medical school, I went to church with every intention not to form long lasting relationships. This worked for a few months, until some of the younger pastors on staff were interested in fostering relationships with students from Christopher Newport University.

I could no longer hide behind attending different services and it didn't help that I preferred sitting in the front. It wasn't to get attention, but more to avoid not being distracted by all the heads in front of me. Of course, as a creature of habit, I sat in the same section and chair every Sunday. Talk about being predictable. I eventually made friends within the congregation and begin to serve with the First Impressions team, where I met one a friend, Kedra. I also plugged myself into the young adult ministry, Refuge. I had been going to church for most of my life. This meant I knew all the right phrases and behaviors to exemplify while on the premises of the church building, but I dared not to let anyone close enough to know that the posture of my heart was not Christ-like. I lifted my hands on Sunday morning singing praises to Jesus as my Lord and Savior, while Monday through Saturday I knowingly sinned. I entertained sexual conversations over the phone, fornicated with more men than I care to recall, did not practice self-control, and explored the party scenes. And at the same time, I would make my faithful appearance to church, to events and even started serving as the United Campus Ministries president on campus. I lived two separate lives, without realizing that the bride of Christ, the Church, is not defined by a building located at a specific address. Because the Holy Spirit lived inside of me, I was carrying the

Church with me everywhere I went. This is not by any means to say the local church is not important. Hebrews 10:25 encourages every believer not to forsake the assembling of ourselves and it is very important that we be part of a local church. *However, as believers we can easily begin to idolize the place of worship we attend, instead of truly reverencing Who we worship.*

Hebrews 4:12 says, "For the word of God is alive and powerful. It is sharper than the sharpest two-edged sword, cutting between soul and spirit, between joint and marrow. It exposes our innermost thoughts and desires" (NLT). Though I had done a good job of being a hypocrite, there is power in God's Word. As I sat through different teachings at Calvary, the Word began to pierce through my heart and expose my wickedness. As I examined how much God had been good to me, I couldn't help but be in a state of repentance. During this sanctification journey, somewhere in November of 2011, my ex flew to Charlotte, North Carolina, to express that he had made a huge mistake in breaking up with me. I remember him attempting to be romantic and me feeling numb to it all. I eventually told him I didn't see a future in us, but that I would think about it. Looking back, I now know I should have stuck to my decision and continued my journey single and in pursuit of the Lord. But like most women, I held on to what once was. I clung to what we could be some day. I held on to the fear of what others would say. I told myself I would go back to him only with one condition. I wanted to do it God's way. I didn't know what that really meant at the time, but I for sure knew I wanted to stop having sex before marriage.

The year 2012 was bound to be a major year. I was scheduled to graduate with a biology degree in May and possibly pursue medical school. As I pondered on my future, I realized that my dream of going to medical school was birthed out of people pleasing. My science course load was brutal, and I often wonder how I managed to graduate on time while working two jobs, managing an emotional rollercoaster love relationship and navigating through the dysfunctionality of the cultural customs of my family. Yet by God's grace, I survived. With a promise made to a deceased father and the signs leading me into education, I found myself in the office of my advisor, Dr. Myers. Dr. Myers was a short Caucasian man who had a strong passion for science and had been at the university for quite some time. I knew I couldn't talk to anyone in my family about this matter as they all expected me to be the next Dr. Kasonga. The few people who I had come to call friends had troubles of their own and ultimately it was my decision to make. As I sat with Dr. Myers and cried about this junction in my life, he looked at me with eyes of a man that had been on earth longer than I and could impart some wisdom. Dr. Myers reassured me that having a Dr. in front of my name did not have to happen by way of medical school immediately. "Njiba, you know oftentimes we think that things in life must happen in ABC order. I have found that oftentimes life has a way of taking you to Z, then D, or K before A, and that's completely okay," he added. These words have echoed in my spirit long after leaving the campus of CNU and I have used them to impart wisdom to others. Dr. Myers concluded with, "If you are passionate about educating children, why don't you take some courses this semester that are related to the field. In the meantime, stick with your biology degree because you have come too far to change it now. I would also encourage you to apply to the Master of Arts in Teaching here at CNU and just see what happens!"

Proverbs 11:14 says, "Where no counsel is, the people fall: but in the multitude of counsellors there is safety" (KJV). Coming from a background where I never saw anyone go to counseling and all our problems were to stay enclosed in our home, I was grateful for my obedience in seeking Dr. Myers' counsel concerning school. I did just as he recommended. I enrolled in education courses that semester, in which I earned A's effortlessly. I applied to the master's program and just so I wouldn't have all my eggs in one basket, I also applied to a program called Teach for America. Though my prayer life was infantile, I boldly told the Lord to only open one door. I didn't want the responsibility of choosing one program over the other and I wanted Him to make it clear which direction I should go. While I consulted my Creator regarding my future concerning school and career, I made little investment in asking Him what I should do concerning my love life. Going back to my ex "felt" right and around April of 2012, I told my ex we could give ourselves a chance again. By this point, we had been communicating on the phone and had seen each other over Valentine's Day. He had helped me purchased my first vehicle, a 2001 Ford Taurus for $2,000, which he ended up driving to Virginia for me. Though we were not officially a couple, he told me it was his responsibility to help me fulfill the goals we had talked about together. Of course, this gave me a sense of security and ultimately hope in him as the provider for our family someday. *I fell in love all over with the potential him instead of the reality him.*

Will you marry me?

On May 12th, 2012, I walked across the stage and received my first degree from Christopher Newport University. I couldn't believe four years of labor went into earning a piece of paper that cost over $80,000 and since I had been accepted in the master's program, I knew that number would be more by August 2013. I was extremely grateful for Dr. Mitchel and his wife to have invested in me for four years. They attended my graduation like proud grandparents and gave me many accolades after the ceremony. God not only made my option simple by closing the door for Teach for America, but He also placed it on Dr. Mitchel's heart to support me through two semesters of graduate school. This was unmerited favor at its best. I was overwhelmed with joy seeing my peers receiving their degrees that day, excited for the future and cherishing all that CNU had allowed us to share. It was a beautiful and joyous day. My adoptive family was present and so was my boyfriend, with friends of ours.

Graduation was a huge deal because it was the first time my adoptive parents were getting the opportunity to meet their potential future son-in-law. All these years, I never addressed the idea of us being together because it was ingrained in us that once the parents knew who the boyfriend was, you couldn't bring anyone else around.

Therefore, you had to be sure this was the person you wanted to spend the rest of your life with. Talk about pressure! I obviously wanted everything that weekend to go smoothly and it did. To avoid my adoptive mom fussing about laboring in the kitchen to celebrate my accomplishment as she did for my high school graduation, I rented the back space of an Asian restaurant. We gathered there after the graduation, and everyone paid for their own $10 meal. It was cost efficient, and no one had to clean up. This was my least favorite part whenever we had any gatherings at the house. After the Asian buffet, my significant other and our friends continued our weekend with other festivities. Everyone spent time at my apartment in the afternoon. Later that night, we went to a club in Virginia Beach and had a blast. The next morning, we had breakfast at my adoptive parents' house for the official meeting of my boyfriend. Thankfully, nothing awkward happened and we went to Virginia Beach afterwards. For the first time ever, I believed that my adoptive parents saw me as an adult. It felt great not to have to ask permission for anything. After all, I conveniently started claiming myself on my taxes my sophomore year of college. This created a big problem for my adoptive mother, since I was clear that neither she nor my adoptive father were providing a minimum of 50 percent of my care. Of course, my adoptive mom revoked my privileges of having a key to her house then and so by 2012, I sincerely felt like a true guest in the house. A drama-free weekend was rare when we all gathered, and I couldn't be any happier that was finally a reality.

I immediately started my graduate courses after graduating with my bachelor's. The master's program was an intensive one year accelerated program. Since I was not on the track for education to begin with, I was scheduled to graduate in August 2013 with a few other latecomers. During that summer, I took courses on campus and enrolled at Phoenix University online so that I could catch up with the credits I needed to graduate on time. With such a demanding schedule, I could no longer work at the I.T. Help Desk on campus, and I barely had time to work the 21st Century program with Newport News Public School. Upon explaining my situation to my boss, Mr. Corey Gordon, who played a tremendous role in my journey as an educator, assured me that he would have me work on a few projects with him remotely and put in some hours in the office to at least help me have a few pennies. I was beyond grateful for his willingness to aid me. Given the pain, the unforgiveness in my heart and pride, I was determined to never ask my adoptive parents for help. I wanted to prove that I could make it without them and didn't need a constant throw in my face of all the things they had done for me. Inadvertently, this mindset and perspective became breeding ground for my reluctance to ask for help and always striving to prove others wrong even if it comes at the cost of living my life to please others.

I plunged into the business of my studies and maintained my long-distance relationship with my significant other. We always found ways to visit each other. We didn't have a rule as to how many months could pass before we had to see each other, but we found a way to make it at least every two to three months depending on what was happening in our lives. While I worked diligently to earn my second degree, he attended community college and worked on having his own business. Though our schedules were hectic, through many disagreements, we found a way to keep the spark. Though I had expressed to him that I no longer wanted to sin against God by having sex, somehow, I always found myself giving in when we saw each other. Then I would go home and cry before God asking Him to forgive me once again. I didn't share my struggle with sexual sin with anyone because sex had always been a taboo subject and sadly, I wasn't enjoying it. There were no climax moments for me. I simply thrived on the perverted viewpoint that men enjoyed it, I could provide it and that was the essence of it all. Yet as a child of the Most High, the Holy Spirit in me did not allow me to enjoy my sin. Instead of repenting and forsaking it though, I hardened my heart towards that part of my life. Christ could have everything else, but concerning sex, I would compromise. I loved the benefits of being associated with Christ and saying I loved Him. Yet my love for Christ without obedience to His Word made a mockery of who I had professed to be.

The year 2012 went by as quickly as it came, and I found myself nearing the end of my program. I spent my mornings doing my student-teaching hours at Dutrow Elementary in a 5th grade class, under the supervision of Mr. Steve Herman. Mr. Herman had been in education for many years and had a passion for learning. He was a tall Caucasian family man with a quiet spirit. We immediately connected on a professional level, and he was willing to teach me all that he could, while allowing me to make mistakes along the way. I fell in love with his class. They were the pioneer to my daily "reasons why I teach" entries. I knew that being a teacher would not be a breeze and that tough days would come. I began journaling all the great things that would take place in class as a reminder on days when I want to quit of the reason why I even started. Amid learning whom I could become professionally, I also met a woman whom I now proudly call mom.

LaShondra Rice was one of the 4th grade teachers at Dutrow. She was an African American woman, married with no children of her own and had a husband who served in the Air Force. For the most part, we exchanged brief conversations on a professional level. She was always well put together from head to toe. She exuded a strength that reminded me of Maman, but I never shared my admiration with her. Being someone who often found myself in male circles and could easily befriend guys, I did not have many women who spoke into my life. My friend Kedra and I were still getting to know each other. Not only was she a mom of two and a principal, but we were also fourteen years apart. While I considered her a friend, I knew she viewed me then as a little sister who reminded her so much of herself and a potential mentee in whom she could impart wisdom. Plus, I genuinely avoided relationships with women. I found them to be too emotional and I shared no common interests with them. I was the girl who played and watched sports. I disliked overly romantic movies and preferred action and comedic movies. I didn't like doing my hair and nails and found talking about guys a boring subject. So, to only have a professional relationship with Mrs. Rice was perfect. All this changed on April 9th, 2013.

It was my twenty-second birthday and I had plans to spend time in my books like usual. Since Papa and Maman had died, no one really took the time to make birthdays special. I grew to expect no birthday wishes or presents. My birthday became a day when I cried because I missed my parents so much. I happened to be at work on my birthday and Mrs. Rice asked me what I would be doing for my birthday, to which I gave the usual nothing answer. She looked at me and said, "Great! I am taking you out to dinner." Perplexed by the invitation, I accepted anyways. If anyone knows me, they know I rarely say no to a free meal. That night we ended up at an Indian restaurant called Nawab. It was my first time having Indian food. As we were seated, she uttered my most hated phrase, "So, tell me about yourself." I despised this phrase because I never knew where to start or what version of the truth, I wanted people to know. And though my heart sank at the thought of being raw, vulnerable, and honest, a voice inside me said it was safe. For the next two hours, I spilled my heart out to her and she just listened. By the end of the night, I still didn't know much about her but when we parted, she said, "God told me to take you out for your birthday. I already knew you didn't have plans. As strange as it may have seemed to you, I had to be obedient to the promptings of the Holy Spirit. Thank you for sharing your birthday with me." Immediately, there was a peace in my spirit. I didn't know where our relationship would go, but in the meantime, I knew the Lord had sent me a woman who would speak into my life professionally, spiritually, and emotionally.

A few days after my birthday, I was offered a job teaching 5th grade at Richneck Elementary, and I hadn't even completed my degree. The Lord has truly given me grace when it comes to employment because I have never had to work hard to acquire any of the positions I have held. I typically walk away from the interview knowing the job is mine, and God has been faithful to provide. Having secured a job in April removed much of my anxiety as far as what I would do when graduate school was over in August. I was able to simply focus on taking the required exams to be licensed in Virginia and satisfying the demands of CNU. With all the hard work and sacrifice I had put in, my significant other decided that we should spend two weeks on the West Coast as soon as my spring semester was over. With the proper motivation, I worked my butt off so I could thoroughly enjoy Las Vegas and Los Angeles. Our relationship had been rocky throughout the whole year, but I was hopeful that this time together would bring us closer. I still struggled with fully trusting that he was in this for the long hall. I was afraid one day he would wake up in a bad mood and decide to throw our relationship away. I even admitted to him when we finally saw each other that I had been withholding myself emotionally for fear of being hurt once again. While all those thoughts bombarded my mind, the traveler in me couldn't wait to finally see these two big cities.

We travelled separately to Las Vegas and met at the airport. We were thrilled to be sharing this first experience together. He had rented a nice car and made reservations at the Paris hotel. Anyone who knows my ex knows appearance and ambiance are big proponents of his being. Like most tourists, we took abundantly too many pictures and posted them on Facebook for the whole world to see. We were empowered by the many likes and comments that applauded us as a power couple, yet inside I knew things were not in order. Our first night, we dressed up and went to dinner in the Eiffel Tower of the hotel. He asked me how I saw our relationship and how I was feeling about our future. For the first time, I was brutally honest and told him we weren't ready. We had too many issues to resolve and quite frankly, I wasn't giving the relationship 100 percent to protect my heart. He acknowledged my concerns and from what I found out later, he immediately realized that proposing that night may not have been the best idea.

With that tough conversation out of the way, I felt free to truly enjoy my much-earned vacation. Vegas was exactly what everyone said it would be: the sin city. The strip was a sight to see, and I was amazed at the amount of people who vacationed there with their children. But hey, to each their own. After enjoying the night life, the pool parties, shopping, and extravagant food, we departed for Los

Angeles where my freshman year suitemate Tara would be our tour guide. We had not seen each other in at least two years, and I was excited to reconnect with her. After graduating from Oregon State, Tara moved to Los Angeles to pursue her acting career. The drive from Vegas to LA was desert dry and uneventful. The traffic was ridiculous, and the trip felt like an all-day marathon. We eventually made it to LA, which had even more traffic than I want to ever remember. Though exhausted, we reunited with Tara and had a blast catching up like we had never spent any time apart. It was Tara's first time meeting my significant other in person and I so wanted to get the girlfriend approval. But with no time for all that, we dove into the itinerary Tara had planned for our three days stay and of course to make things more pleasant, mother nature decided it was the perfect time for my period to start. As a heavy bleeder then, this meant I would be miserable for most of the trip. *Yet when you suffer from people pleasing syndrome, you smile to hide the pain at the expense of your own health.*

We visited beaches, famous parks, neighborhood, restaurants and all that Los Angeles had to offer. During one of our lunches, Tara probed concerning my future with my boyfriend. I remember telling her that we had come a long way and I felt as though this trip was a way for us to rebuild. Having information that I wasn't privileged to, Tara simply nodded and kept up with other conversations. It was a beautiful July day, and I was so busy enjoying the breeze of LA that I never picked up on any cues. I had not realized that Tara and my boyfriend had been communicating via text. I was not one to snoop on his phone although I knew I had access to it. Therefore, I was oblivious to everything happening around me. Later that day, a friend of mine whom I call Bestie Loko, a nickname he earned while we drank Four Loko joined us with his girlfriend. It was a pleasure to meet her, and I was astonished by how good of a time we all were having. Tara planned for us to end the day at Griffith Park. Griffith Park is one of the largest municipal parks with urban wilderness areas in the United States. It is in the eastern Santa Monica Mountain range with a beautiful view of Los Angeles and the sunset. It was breath taking.

As we walked around the park, simply exploring, we finally stopped just to take in the view. I stood there looking at the sun in awe at God's creation and the fact that I was blessed with the opportunity to witness such a sight. Then I felt my boyfriend's hand around my waist as he whispered sweet words in my ear. "Laura, you know I love you. We have been through a lot over these last four years, but I told you from the beginning I would make you my wife and the mother of my children." At this point my heart was beating fast and I was annoyed because the last thing I wanted him to do during this trip was to propose. He got on his knee and asked, "Njiba, will you marry me?" This was probably another's girl dream, but it was not mine. I immediately ran the opposite way and then realized we were in public. I looked up and this was happening. He was still there on his knee waiting for my response. I had specifically told him in our previous conversations that I didn't want a public proposal. I preferred something small with just the two of us and my only requirement was that he plan for someone to capture the moment. He had the people to capture the moment but failed to follow through with my ideal private proposal. All of this was going through my head as I ran away from him. Then in a blink of an eye, I heard the crowd awing and clapping. I didn't have the guts to say no in front of all these people I had never met. I ran back towards him, stuck my hand out, let him put the ring on my finger and hugged him. I never uttered that I would marry him and that should have been indicating signs of where we were heading in the near future.

Not convinced by my theatrics, he later asked if I was happy to be engaged to him. I had spent the first hour since our engagement sending pictures to people who mattered to me, or those I thought should know before I made it social media official. I was even bold and sent a message to my adoptive parents despite knowing that the cultural protocol had been breached. For our family, it was expected that an official presentation should take place prior to an engagement ring being given. I quickly responded by assuring him that I was happy, but I was also shocked. I told him I didn't expect him to propose especially with all the fights and arguments we had leading up to the trip. I expressed that I was taken aback by the fact that it was in such a public place. He defended himself by saying it made for a romantic environment and at least he made sure someone was there to capture the moment. The sad part about this is I found out later that he didn't have a plan for proposing. He left the production to Tara and had she not intervened, he would have been proposing on the day my menstrual cramps were horrid.

Pain in Pleasure

It's amazing how you can't imagine your life without someone and yet when they are no longer in your life, it's like all the pieces of the puzzle finally make sense. I left the East Coast as a recent graduate looking forward to what life would have to offer and I left the West Coast with a fiancé, not knowing what that truly meant. As a young girl, I never took time to envision my ideal wedding. After all the events that took place with my abuser, my violator and every word curse spoken over my life, I was convinced that no man would want me. Yet here I was having to think about planning a wedding. My significant other and I had agreed that I would finish my last few classes, work for a year to get experience and then join him where he was. During all of that, we would plan to do all the formalities to satisfy our customs. According to Congolese customs, there are multiple steps to becoming husband and wife. First, the guy comes to the house with his friends and family to do what is called the presentation. Essentially, this is where he makes his intentions known and receives the dowry lists. The second phase is the actual dowry or traditional wedding. In this ceremony, the women's family would have asked for certain material things such as suits, African fabrics, drinks, food, goat, and money. This is a gift that the guy would bring as a token of appreciation to the woman's family for raising her and as his way of sealing the deal that she now belonged to him. For some families, the dowry would be enough for them to be considered a married a couple, and some couples choose to live together afterwards. If not, then they would perform the civil wedding at the Justice of the Peace, followed by a religious ceremony.

To be frank, while I love most things about the Congolese culture, this marital ceremonial processes just seemed a bit overboard to me. However, I wouldn't dare say anything because I wanted to follow the rules. I wanted everyone else to be happy and proud of me. Therefore, my significant other and I began to discuss timelines after our summer 2013 vacation. We chose to have the presentation in January of 2014 and the dowry in the summer of that same year. Then, I would move in with him and together we would plan our religious ceremony. While I was not fond of all the steps, I requested that we get married by my pastor, Tony Clark, and go through premarital counseling. My significant other professed himself to be a Christian and claimed to have accepted Him as his Lord and Savior. Yet, he had no local church to call his own, no spiritual disciplines that I witnessed and no bearing fruits to show any connectivity to the vine, Christ. Similarly, my walk with Christ was not constant and I was not in a place to remove the speck from his eye. So, I chose to insert spiritual matters as much as I could without becoming the spiritual leader of our relationship. By this point we were five years in, we had fornicated, shared finances and our deepest secrets. Our lives were so intertwined without God's hand of approval, but I was determined like Rebekah to somehow deceive God into thinking I was deserving of Esau's blessing!

"You have become too spiritual," my partner would often say, and anytime I was not in agreement with his proposals he would utter, "Is this what they are teaching you at church?" Understanding that there was obviously a strong disconnect with where we stood on faith, I just stopped sharing that part of my life with him. Eventually, the 2013–2014 academic year began, and I became super busy with attempting not to drown as a first-year teacher. I had become more involved at Calvary Chapel and created a support system to grow in my sanctification journey. My partner being miles away started working night shifts, which caused a breach in our communication. By the time he was heading in to work, I was too tired to be on the phone, and while I was up, rejuvenated, heading to work, he could barely hold a conversation. The distance and infrequent contact soon became our realities. Neither he nor I felt like our relationship was the same or that it would even survive. Nonetheless, there was a wedding in Raleigh, North Carolina, we would both be attending in November, and we looked forward to reconnecting.

After three months since our wonderful vacation and engagement, we were finally in the same room again. While I was excited to see him, once again we had been arguing over the last few weeks and my heart was becoming tired. Though we had traveled with other friends, we were eventually able to have some time alone. I remember picking up his phone casually and looking through it. As much as I would like to say I was surprised, I wasn't. I found messages and pictures that a fiancé shouldn't find. Being the mellow person that I am, I simply asked the question everyone asks, "Who is she?" This wasn't the first time I had found things that were not conducive for someone in a relationship, and I honestly thought that now that he had publicly told the world he would marry me this wouldn't happen again. I had only fooled myself. Finding things on the phone was not the worst part. What made it worse was that he justified himself by saying, "Well, you have become too busy for me. We are miles apart; what do you expect me to do?" I stood there with no words, no emotions, and a clouded mind. "Let's make the best of this weekend," I responded. I did exactly just that. I had become a professional pretender by now. I stood by him throughout the weekend and smiled. Everyone from the outside saw a power couple, who had withstood distance, a breakup and were now on the come up to seal the deal with our vows. Internally, I despised this false picture I was portraying, but I also loved the accolade and applause of men. *This was the perfect recipe for failure because no applause of men is worth the disapproval of God.* Yet while the pleasures of sin may be temporary, they are still pleasurable. I indulged in the lie, hypocrisy, and deceit. When the festivities were over and prior to my departure, I looked at him and told him I needed a break. I needed to spend time praying about us and he said he supported me one hundred percent.

I took the month of December to really reflect on our relationship. On one hand, my partner was scheduled to come meet my adoptive parents in January to officially ask for my hand in marriage. On the other hand, I was not sure if this was the road I wanted to head down. I didn't have many people who I could share my struggles with because I didn't want advice that was shallow. I finally broke down and shared with Mrs. Rice about my internal conflict. By this time, I claimed her as my godmother, and she had left me in charge of one of the sites for her after-school program. I knew I could trust her with my emotional mess. Mrs. Rice never told me what to do. She pointed me back to the Word of God and asked me to consider at what cost I was willing to make this relationship work. To someone who despised failure, I was willing to give everything. But not so I could genuinely be happy in my relationship, but so I wouldn't become the failure I was once told I would be. Since Mrs. Rice was more of a mom to me, I decided to run things through Kedra. Kedra knew my dirt and loved me anyway. I knew she had my back but wouldn't shy away from telling me the truth in love. And like Mrs. Rice, she didn't tell me what to do. She simply said, "Njiba you can't force yourself to love or be loved." Her words echoed through my head many days as I wondered if he would choose me over the others or was I just part of a picture-perfect couple image we had created. After what seemed like weeks of no contact, I told my significant other it was okay for him to come do the presentation. I honestly did not know what I would tell my adoptive parents and couldn't imagine the embarrassment I would feel if I told them things were cancelled.

The year 2014 came and I would be turning twenty-three that year. I had two degrees under my belt, a career, a man and on track to be married. My adoptive mom was kind enough to prepare a few things to host my significant other. A few of my adoptive siblings had managed to clear their schedules to be present. My adoptive dad's only request was that he, my significant other, not show up by himself because this is a family matter. Unfortunately, my partner chose not to adhere to such protocol and came by himself. We proceeded with the customary dialogues and discussed that the dowry would happen in the summer of 2014. With his stay being short, I had scheduled for us to complete our first premarital counseling appointment. Though I had wanted Pastor Tony to do our wedding, I was informed that he no longer did counseling with congregants, but that Pastor Tito would do it. Pastor Tito was one of the assistant pastors on staff. He had been at Calvary for about three years at this point. I did not know him well, but we had a few exchanges in the church lobby. One of the longest conversations we ever had, was in August of 2013 when I had a very vivid dream. Though I had always been a dreamer, given the mockery I had received previously concerning dreams, I had stopped discussing them with others. However, I knew that some of my dreams came to pass and had significance to them. So, when I dreamed of being in a room full of diplomats and other dignitaries, being the only one holding the key to a door, I knew I needed to talk with someone. I remember asking one of the ladies at the church who the prophetic voice in the church was or if there was someone who understood dreams, and she told me to see Pastor Tito. Pastor Tito shared the interpretation of the dream, gave me Scriptures, and shared books with me that I never cracked open till years later. I held on to his words, "Njiba, the anointing on your head is to be amongst kings and queens," and he wasn't the first person to give me words that affirmed that I was destined for more.

My partner and I met with Pastor Tito for about an hour. My significant other didn't find the importance in doing premarital counseling, since we had made it this far without it. Yet for me we seemed to be hanging by a thread. During our session, Pastor Tito told us both that it would be difficult for him to continue counseling us since my partner did not live in Newport News. He gave us the premarital manuals and asked us to spend time doing the homework. If we had any questions, we could call him and discuss. He also took a good portion of our time to ask us questions about our view of marriage and where our walks with the Lord were. Based on the few questions he asked, Pastor Tito recommended that my partner find a local church where he could be fed spiritually and hopefully come back for another face-to-face session. This was my partner's first- and last-time setting foot on the premises of Calvary Chapel Newport News, as far as I know.

He returned to his hometown, and I began applying for jobs there to officially join him that summer. I never received a call for an interview and was very discouraged by the lack of job opportunity. Meanwhile, my significant other was living in a one-bedroom apartment with his brother and working diligently to make progress in his business. Though I was not fond of living in a big city, I was willing to move if I had at least the job security. From his departure in January to March of 2014, I kept asking him questions about his plans for getting a new place. I did not want to be a newlywed couple living in a one bedroom with his brother. There were never any concrete answers on his part, just that he was working on things. I was also adamant about him finding a local church for us to attend together once I moved. I had given him recommendations that were suggested to me by people in the faith, but church did not seem like a priority to him at this time. In addition, he had many stressors from being a new business owner and trying to make a profit. When I examined all these things, I just didn't think me moving there was the best idea. I suggested that he move up to Newport News, but he knew that couldn't happen since he was finally living in a big city like he had always wanted to. I felt stuck.

On Sunday, March 30th, 2014, I walked into the lobby of Calvary Chapel defeated. Even though I had been attending for years, many people did not know what truly went on in my personal life. I had developed a relationship with Pastor Tony and Mrs. Jenise, who were like parents to me, but I did not run to them with every detail of my problems. They were both sad at the thought of me moving to be with my fiancé but were going to respect my decision. Mama J as I called her made sure when my significant other visited that she grilled him with as many questions as a mom could ask in a short amount of time. They had my best interest at heart. Of course, my now bestie Kedra knew how I felt, and she continuously prayed for me. Yet on that specific Sunday, the mask I had mastered wearing to hide the pain could no longer hold the weight of my heart. Pastor Tito was in the lobby and being the discerning man that he is, came to ask if I was okay. I really wanted to lie to him but for some reason lying to someone who did our premarital counseling did not seem right. So, I just came out and told him.

"Pastor Tito, I am struggling. I am engaged. I honestly don't want to move because things aren't lining up and I am not sure how to even have this conversation with him." Pastor Tito being who he is, asked me a series of questions that were all backed up by Scriptures and let the Word of God marinate in my spirit. "Njiba, I can't tell you what to do. But what I can tell you is this, if you are agonizing this much, you must not be at peace. God is not the author of confusion. Christ came so you could have life abundantly and He says in John 14:27 that He left us His peace. The Bible urges us in Ephesians 4:15 to speak the truth in love. You need to at least let your fiancé know what you are feeling and thinking. Let me pray with you." I walked away from the conversation feeling encouraged, but terrified. I went to the sanctuary and cried my eyes out during worship. I just wanted God to tell me exactly what I needed to do and do it for me. Unfortunately, and fortunately, God did not create us as robots. He gave us a free will and the ability to choose Him, His path, and His commands. I knew I was His sheep, but I wasn't sure if in this moment I was hearing His voice.

April 1st is typically the day people fool each other and somewhere during the conversation, they retract their words and say, "April fools!" Unfortunately, for my partner there was no April fool's joke. I asked him if he could carve out some time for us to talk about us. During our conversation, I expressed to him that I was not willing to move in with him without having secured a job. I articulated that there were still things he was attempting to put in place and that we could use the extra year to figure things out. I wanted us to proceed with doing the dowry in the summer, except I wouldn't be moving until 2015. While on the phone, nothing seemed to have caught my significant other by surprise. He understood where I was coming from, and we discussed every matter like two responsible adults. I went to bed feeling lighter and thankful we had cleared the air! But if you've noticed anything about my life, you should know that pain tends to befriend me often.

I woke up the next morning to a text from him saying, "When there are clouds in the sky, it's likely to rain. I can tell where this is headed. Laura, you have never loved me, nor do you love me. If you truly did, it wouldn't matter if I had a job, a place or anything else. You would move down here because you love me." I had barely taken the crusty boogers out of my eyes and now I was being accused of not loving him. I honestly did not know how to respond. I attempted to defend myself by telling him he was being unreasonable and that my decision not to move down was not permanent. It was a temporary sacrifice while we both got things in order. I believe that's wisdom. He didn't want to hear any of that. Out of his own pain, frustration, pride or whatever he was feeling then, he lashed out multiple text messages that were unpleasant. I personally did not have the mental, emotional, or spiritual fortitude to fight this battle. So, to everything he sent, I simply said OKAY. I told him if he was choosing to believe I didn't love him, I couldn't make him see otherwise and I didn't have the energy to fight. We went back and forth via text multiple times until I had enough. I told him my spring break was coming up and I could come see him so we could discuss things in person. He told me that wouldn't be necessary, and he didn't need me breaking up with him in person.

My cooperative teacher Mr. Herman taught me to never make decisions while I am angry. He told me to always sleep and examine the situation the next day. I don't think my partner had considered the weight of his words. Spring break came and I spent it somewhere else, which made him more upset at me. He used me not coming as proof and justification of his claim that I didn't love him. I had refused to be manipulated and told him if he had wanted me there, he should have said so. The back and forth was becoming exhausting. I recall Pastor Tito calling me a few days into the month of April to see how I was doing. I shared with him how having an open dialogue had caused a turn of events and this time I believed we were done for good. I had dreamed for almost five years of our lives together. We had picked out baby names and envisioned getting old together. All of it came crumbling down at my choice to express how I truly felt about moving. I really wanted to feel pain, but I felt numb. I was in solution mode. How could I undo this bed that I had made and had to lay in for the rest of the world to see?

Months passed and I finally had to tell my adoptive parents that there wouldn't be a dowry. Their response to the matter scared me for months. My adoptive mother was quick to tell me that this was the result of me choosing to sleep with family members. My sins were too deep, and all my relationships would end in divorce. These were the last words I needed to hear amid being wounded. Everything was always my fault. I spared them any details and continued about my journey of dissociating myself from being the future "Mrs." It started with taking off the ring, slowly removing pictures on Facebook and then finally acknowledging that I was no longer engaged. Though I was no longer engaged in status and my lips could utter that truth, my heart was engaged in a dysfunctional understanding of love. It would take the reckless love of God and His Word to untangle my long-lasting affair with the cares of the world.

CHAPTER 7: THE DOVE

The Altar

In Matthew 10 Jesus calls His disciples and sends them out for ministry. He gives them the authority to drive out impure spirits and to heal every sickness and disease. In verse 16 He tells them, "I am sending you out like sheep among wolves. Therefore, be wise as serpents and harmless as doves" (NKJV), and at this juncture of my life I felt as though the wolves were devouring me. The little wisdom I thought I had was not getting me anywhere and I found myself on my knees crying out to God. Nothing in my past or present felt harmless as a dove, yet the Holy Spirit was drawing me near and like Jacob, I wrestled with God.

Though I had grown in my relationship with Christ, I was still walking the fence. I knew being a Christian would not make me sinless, but the power of the Gospel is enough to make us sin LESS. 1 Corinthians 6:12 tells us that "All things are lawful, but all things are not profitable. All things are lawful for me, but I will not be brought under the power of any" (NKJV). The unfortunate part for me in my walk with Christ was that the major sin that I could call out in my life was not even permissible for me. Having been exposed to sex at a young age, I found myself struggling with promiscuity, not because I thoroughly enjoyed what took place in fornication, but simply because giving my body to a man became the standard. I could walk into a room and know exactly whose number I could get, whom I could have sex with and whom I would simply entertain conversation with. I took no pleasure in the sexual act but thrived on this egotistic string of being wanted and knowing so.

The Bible says obedience is better than sacrifice (1 Samuel 15:22), and I have never regretted the times I have obeyed God's Word. Disobedience to God's Word is heartbreaking and will have your promised land right under your nose but you can't see it. By one man's disobedience, sin entered the world, and by one horny and perverted young man's choice, my sexual immoralities led me to 40 years in the desert. Of course, not literally 40 years, but I have had enough sexual encounters that I am not proud of. Looking back, it's hard to know if I would have remained a virgin until marriage. Quite frankly, I don't know, nor will I ever know. What I do know is when I look back at the wickedness of my heart and the sexual impurities I allowed my body to experience, whether forcefully or as willing participant, my heart aches. My heart aches because God's design for sex within the confines of marriage is ultimately the best plan. The sacrifices I made in being rebellious or promiscuous to be accepted, or to fill a void through sexual acts outside of marriage have all become painful memories. To know now that I had accepted Christ in my heart and the Holy Spirit was living inside me, yet I was grieving it, causes me to wonder how much I missed out on growing my intimacy with the Lord. *But when you don't know better, you don't do better. And sometimes when you do know better, you still don't do better.* I can recall many days and nights on my knees asking God to forgive me one more time for my sin. Interesting enough, it never got easier with time because time alone in itself simply does not heal.

With a failed engagement behind me, I was determined to not repeat the same mistakes moving forward. Yet amid attempting to walk in purity I missed the mark often. There were many gentlemen wanting to make me their woman, and I turned them down. Others I passionately lusted after thinking I was in love, only to be rejected by them and realize I had wasted my time. The year 2014 was coming to an end and I knew I needed to stop loving my sin. I was twenty-four with a future ahead of me, and I was eager to see what living a life truly surrendered to God would entail for me. Despite my disobedience, my trials and circumstances, God had provided for me. His goodness towards me could only lead me to repentance—repentance of heart, mind, body, and soul. By the washing of the Word and fellowship among other believers, I found healing in knowing God had forgiven me and that everything was covered under the blood of Christ. Therefore, living a life of purity would not come out of my own doing and behavior modification. I finally realized that the more I pressed into Christ, the less I enjoyed what God hates. I became more aware of the price of being reconciled to God. Jesus had to be wounded so I could win. There was freedom in the shedding of His blood and His resurrection. However, I did not walk in the freedom because walking by sight was easier than walking by faith.

CHAPTER 8: READY OR NOT

Specialist

"Pastor Tito, I just don't want to deal with relationships anymore." This was the only thing I could take away from all the emotional madness I had been experiencing in 2014. Pastor Tito just smiled and reassured me that I was only twenty-three years old with many years ahead of me. "Njiba, you can't make everyone else suffer because other relationships did not work out. Think about this, let's say you get married at forty and stay alive to be ninety. You would have been married for fifty years! That's quite a long time. Give yourself a break."

After doing a long-distance relationship for six years, I knew for sure I did not want that again. I sometimes thought of the prayer I prayed the first time my ex-fiancé broke up with me while we were dating. I told God that when He sent me my husband, I wanted to meet him Monday, date him Tuesday, be engaged Wednesday, do the presentation and dowry Thursday, the civil wedding Friday, the religious wedding Saturday and off to our honeymoon Sunday. It seemed like a ridiculous prayer, and I even jokingly shared it with those close to me. But I would forget about that prayer and my desire to be married, especially with all that had happened. Yet there were many guys who pursued me. I would entertain the conversations, but I knew I did not want the relationships to go any further. This was true until I met Specialist.

Through mutual friends, I had befriended a Congolese girl whom I became close to. I would travel to see her and her family. We got along well, but we weren't ones to play matchmaker for each other. She had told me she had a cousin who was in the Army whom I had never met but that was soon to change in December of 2014. Around the third week of December, we had received word that one of my relatives who was only twenty years old had been admitted to the hospital in intensive care. I was shocked by the news since I had just seen her earlier in the month of December to celebrate her birthday. I along with my adoptive sisters left Virginia a few days later and headed to the hospital. Sadly, we would be spending Christmas in the hospital. Things were not looking good at all. With many stores and restaurants closed on Christmas day, my friend who lived near the hospital said I could come spend the evening with her family so I could at least get some food. I rarely say no to free food; it's the way to my stomach and unfortunately, not my heart.

Upon my arrival, her family was sympathetic, and many asked about how we were holding up. I noticed a guy in an Army uniform and concluded this was the cousin I had never met. He was dark-skinned, shorter than I prefer, and very courteous. He offered me his seat, took my coat, and made small talk. Being that I had been around the family before, I was comfortable. I ate as if I was in my home, laughed at the jokes and indulged in their family's good time. It was better than spending time in the hospital. After the festivities, I said my goodbyes and thanked the family for their generosity. Little did I know, I became the topic of discussion for my friend's cousin. Unfortunately, my friend was not fond of hooking up her family members with her friends because when things didn't work out, relationships became awkward. Since he couldn't get information about me from her, he asked her sister. She told the little that she knew: "She is a teacher. She was engaged but it didn't work. She has a master's degree." At least that was what Specialist later told me. Thanks to Facebook, he really did not have to work hard to get in touch with me.

We immediately connected through our sense of humor while chatting online and unlike what I would typically do, I gave him my number so we could communicate if I was not on Facebook. From then on, we became virtually inseparable. I knew I would be coming back to visit my relative at the hospital on New Year's and he insisted that he take me out on a date. Pastor Tito's words of giving guys a chance echoed in my head and I said, "Why not?" We had a fantastic day together and talked until we couldn't keep our eyes open. He was a gentleman the entire day and the night even ended with a kiss. It was 2015 and I had made a promise to God that I wouldn't fornicate anymore. It was January 1st, and I couldn't ruin the resolution already. It helped that I was not all that physically attracted to him. I never dated a guy his height and while it's very superficial, I wasn't falling head over heels based on his looks. He charmed me with his character, and I figured maybe the physical attraction would come later.

Specialist was only home for a short time and then was sent for two months of training. Here I was doing the long-distance thing again and I despised myself for it. We weren't officially boyfriend and girlfriend, but we were committed to getting to know each other. We talked about how we could see a future together, but I was always reluctant on those conversations. I felt it was too soon for me to think that far into the future. Let's take things slowly. By February 2015, he was graduating and had received orders for South Korea. I knew doing long distance within states was hard, and I was not equipped to do a relationship over continents. But since we were friends, we said we would stay in touch. He flew me in for his graduation. We had a great time together. I remember laying in the bed together, both of us almost giving in to sexual temptation, but he looked at me and said, "you said you wanted to wait. Don't break that promise." I knew then he was the real deal. My level of respect for him increased.

The next few months were a struggle. My relative passed away after three months in the hospital and a few weeks in hospice. It was a devastating time for the entire family. I remember funerals taking place while I was young but did not realize everything that went into planning one until I had to be part of making one a reality. Yet through the difficulty of mourning, Specialist was there virtually to comfort and encourage me. We had found ways to utilize Facebook, Skype, Viber, WhatsApp and even Kakao to stay as connected as possible despite the time difference. He became the person I looked forward to hearing when I woke up and when I went to sleep. I eventually introduced him to a few of my relatives, and I gradually met other members of his family. During all these changes, I was also accepted at Regent University for their Education Specialist program and would be scheduled to start classes fall of 2015. The program would take two years and would allow me to be endorsed in administration and supervision for Pre-K through 12th grade. I was not fond of having to take out loans nor did I know how I would manage working full time, running an afterschool program, serving in leadership at church and playing flag football for two different teams on the weekend. But I had a niche for overloading my plate and I seemed to function better this way until my body eventually crashed.

Specialist was always supportive of my dreams and goals. One thing I had on the to-do list that I had yet done was to return my engagement ring to my ex-fiancé and to finally take my name off his Sprint account. I had tried to sell the ring and they weren't offering much. I had also attempted to take care of Sprint, but they kept insisting we needed to both be present. The last time I had seen my ex was January 2014. An entire year had passed and neither one of us had received the proper closure that was needed. A few months after the heat of our argument died down, I heard he was seeing someone already and had deleted me off his Facebook. I still had his number and I contacted him about coming to his town during my summer break so we could put things in order. I chose to stay with my cousin and catch up with her as well. I was nervous to see him after this much time had passed, but I knew this chapter of my life was sealed. Though Specialist was not fond of this trip, he respected my wishes to make it happen.

My ex picked me up for lunch and it was as if time really had not passed. I had known this man since I was seventeen years old. He practically saw me grow into the woman I had become. We had shared so many experiences together that it would be hard for either one of us to lack a topic of conversation. While having lunch, I wondered if people around us could even tell we had not seen each other in over a year. Thankfully, we were able to discuss how we got to where we were. We both concluded that distance, miscommunication, and pride got the best of both of us, but that we wanted nothing but good things for each other. We shared a meal, handled Sprint and I returned his ring to him once he dropped me off. I felt like a weight had been lifted off my shoulders once more. Having difficult conversations was not my strongest suit and because this had gone so well, I thought I was making progress in this part of "adulting." I thought I was becoming more in tune with my emotions and could articulate truthfully how I felt. But I was wrong.

New Dreams

Upon on my return from my visit with my ex, Specialist was hard at work trying to establish himself in his career in the Army. It had been five months since we had seen each other in person, and we were both getting antsy about not having physical contact. Specialist decided he would ask for leave during the month of August and I would travel to South Korea to visit him. I loved the thought of the adventure and couldn't wait to make the trip a reality. As we waited in anticipation for the powers that be to approve or reject his leave, our friendship and relationship grew deeper. I began to fall more and more for his personality. I would envision myself being a military spouse. After all, Mommy LaShondra made it seem feasible and with many couples in Hampton Roads in the Armed Forces, I figured I had plenty of role models. Yet during these new hopes and dreams, I was tormented by the idea that all of this wasn't what I wanted. I had shared with Specialist that I didn't want to be in a relationship, especially not a long-distance one. I had communicated that I wasn't sure if the military life would be for me. The thought of him being gone for months and the possibility of death on the battlefield terrified me. Yet while I knew all these truths, instead of not investing emotionally, I stayed connected to him. I kept coming back. Coming back for the comfort of having a friend, someone who was interested in me and was actively pursuing me. He made me feel wanted, cherished, and loved. He knew he wanted to make me not only his girlfriend, but hopefully one day his wife.

We eventually found out that his leave was denied, but I had already scheduled that time off in August. Instead of just marinating on the sad news, he suggested that I go to Canada to visit his father. I had never been to Canada. It was closer and cheaper than going to South Korea. Yet before I could wrap my mind around meeting his dad, we finally had the talk. He expressed how much he cared about me and that there was no other female he was entertaining. He asked if I had been seeing anyone else and I laughed because with all the things on my plate, I couldn't entertain anyone else. With that in mind he said, "Will you be my girl?" I did not want to disappoint him, nor did I want to lose on the opportunity to be in a relationship with such a great guy. I took a deep breath and slowly said yes. I could see that all the candles in his heart were lit as the biggest smile came across his face. He was happy; therefore, I was happy, right? Typical memo for a people-pleasing gal.

I went to Canada as his girlfriend and had an exceptional time hanging with his dad. Growing up in a household where I didn't have a relationship with any father on an emotional level, I was very skeptical about this whole plan. Specialist reassured me that his dad was the coolest Congolese guy, and I can attest that he truly was. He was my tour guide, took me out to eat, rode rollercoasters with me and so much more. I felt like a little girl having a daddy and daughter date, except this one lasted a week. Sadly, during that trip, Specialist and I had our first miscommunication. I can't remember what it was about, but I know it was my fault. I remember him being disappointed, yet his initial reaction was to understand and know how I felt. I had never had a man who wasn't ready to run at the first sign of my flaws and he chose to bathe me in his affection despite it all. It was mind-blowing. Of course, this didn't help me feeling as though I really shouldn't have said yes to him. So, I bottled up my thoughts and emotions inside. This had cost me in my previous relationship and still, I had not learned that the fundamental part of any relationship is honest communication.

Upon my return from Canada, I embarked on a year of newness. It was year three of teaching and I seemed to have found a groove. With the stable income and me finally deciding to honor God with the first fruits of my labor, I had finally been able to buy a new car. It was a 2015 Honda Civic, and I couldn't believe I walked out with it, not needing a co-signer or a down payment. My classes at Regent had begun with brutality and I could not envision this two-year program coming to an end. Relationally, I was disconnected from many of the relationships I had entertained throughout college, and the paths of people whom I had considered my closest friends seemed to diverge with mine. Spiritually, I was sensing myself drifting from my place of worship, Calvary Chapel. I loved the people, and it was home, but I started not connecting with the sermons as much. I thought it was maybe because I had many things to juggle, so I decided to serve less to just get ministered to. The church was growing, and they were campaigning to get a bigger building. I was tithing and giving above my tithes. Prior to stepping back, I was serving in every capacity I could without burning out and attending worship regularly. My relationships were solid in and outside the church. So much so that Mrs. Jenise Clark even mentioned to Pastor Tony and Pastor Tito one day that I would make such a great pastor's wife! I gasped for air and knew this was far from my dreams. I could never seem to get away from this pastoral life calling. My mind felt clouded. Instead of trying to sort it all, I simply lived each day one minute at a time, praying and hoping I was making the wisest choice.

Property lines

"I don't think I gave you my best yes" was how I finally started the conversation with Specialist. He didn't know what I was trying to say, nor did I know exactly what I wanted to communicate. I attempted to explain to him that it seemed as if I had said "yes" to his request of being his girlfriend from a dishonest place. Being the awesome gentleman that he is, he was more concerned with my fears and apprehensions than the fact that I was causing a breach between us. We made it past this hard conversation and decided to take things one day at a time.

The academic year 2015–2016 began that September and I was excited for the new students I would be teaching. Teaching is by far the most demanding profession ever, yet it is also very rewarding. Teaching had also given me the opportunity to meet kids from all walks of life—the gifted, the average kids and those who have special needs. I suppose this is what allowed Pastor Tito to think of me when he and his wife Traci were going on a cruise. Together they have a son named Christian who has been diagnosed with autism and cerebral palsy. As an active ten-year-old, Pastor Tito thought it would be wise that someone come to their house to relieve his elderly mother-in-law for a few hours while they were gone. Being the helper that I am, I said I wouldn't mind at all. Though I had been at the same church with Pastor Tito, I really didn't know much about his family. I briefly if ever spoke to Traci and I had never had an interaction with Christian. Pastor Tito suggested that I come to the house to see where they lived and meet Christian and his grandmother.

I pulled up at their house, which was in a newly developed neighborhood. The house looked huge from the outside and walking inside proved it to be so. Pastor Tito opened the door when I rang the bell. He was very brief. He asked me to take my shoes off and come into their kitchen. Traci was sitting at the dining room table, while her mom stood at the kitchen sink. They were both petite women and were mostly cordial. Pastor Tito made the quick introduction and then disappeared. Traci decided to tell me a little more about Christian. She shared his likes and dislikes. She told me about what behaviors to expect from him. She walked me through the entire house. I knew I would only be at their house for a few hours, yet it felt like I was getting more than just a tour. The house was beautiful and bare. I figured with a special needs child it was probably best to not have a cluttered home. Traci expressed how the house had been built recently and wasn't even a year old. As we walked up the flight of stairs, Traci kept taking deep breaths. I wasn't sure if she was out of shape or something else was aching her. We finally made it to the landing, and she showed me Christian's room. Like most of the house, Christian's room was spacious yet mostly empty. We then made our way to the third floor, also known as Pastor Tito's man cave. Many of the doors were locked as they did not want Christian to barge into rooms and mess up anything. After the upstairs tour, Traci asked Christian if he wanted to come outside with us to catch bugs. We headed outside and Christian ran away excited at the thought of bugs. Traci then expressed that her back was hurting. Unaware of her condition, I asked her if she had considered getting a massage. She briefly said no but would think about doing so. As we walked in the yard, she showed me where the property line stopped. She expressed how she hoped to do something with the little land that was full of trees but wasn't sure if the city would approve. As I stood there, I wondered if this was their typical procedure whenever anyone helped with watching Christian. The entire meeting time didn't feel as though Traci was making me familiar with her home. It felt as though she was passing on the baton, but I wasn't sure to what yet. As she told Christian it was time to go back inside, Christian threw himself on the grass and started throwing a tantrum. I had never seen a ten-year-old throw a tantrum, but to witness it on a child with special needs made me question if I was ready for the job. Then without hesitation, Traci looked at me and said, "You have to get him."

I forcefully picked up Christian as he demonstrated aggressive behaviors. I had not been trained on properly holding a child his size, but I was able to get him back in the house. This was the last time I saw Traci. She and Pastor Tito left for their cruise while I spent the next couple days bonding with Christian and his grandmother. Though in her seventies, she didn't allow my presence to give her rest. We spent the time I was there getting to know each other. She said I reminded her of her grandkids. She was very transparent with me and truly appreciated me being there. As the week progressed, Christian managed to even call me mom. I knew he didn't mean it and was probably missing his mom. After all, most of my 5th graders called me mom once or twice throughout the academic year. I simply gave him some extra love as we watched a movie together. The week flew by and before I knew it, the Tirados were back. I sent a picture I took with Christian to Pastor Tito with a message saying, "Thank you for the opportunity to hang out with him. Hope you had a great trip." He simply responded with, "Thanks for your help." This was our last communication in September of 2015.

October 2015 came around and I had not seen Pastor Tito at church like normal. But I didn't give it much thought. Specialist and I continued to talk despite the tough conversation we had had about my lack of interest in a long-distance relationship. Then one morning while on a prayer call with a sister from church, she informed me of the unimaginable. Traci Tirado had died on Thursday, October 15, but she did not want a lavish funeral. I had heard she had been diagnosed with cancer, but I did not know how severe it was. I had just seen her in September. I froze as my heart ached for Pastor Tito, Christian and Traci's mom. I had a flashback to my own childhood. I remember Papa getting the news of Maman's death and how devastating this was for him. I recall the heartache I endured later in life having lost my covering. I couldn't even fathom what could possibly be going through Christian's mind. I never know exactly what to say to someone who is grieving, so I tend to say nothing. By Sunday, Pastor Tony had planned to do a service of tribute to Traci to give the congregation an opportunity to empathize with pastor Tito. There was only a few select people in the church who knew Traci had cancer. According to Pastor Tito, she did not want to be defined by cancer and was willing to serve others until she no longer could.

I dreaded Sunday and chose to attend the 8:00 AM service to avoid the crowd. The atmosphere that morning was somber even though worship went on as usual. Many people did not know what was about to happen. Yet after the last worship song, Pastor Tony took the stage and announced that we had lost a member of our congregation. Pastor Tito was sitting up front and looked as if he had been crying all day long. My heart ached watching him grieve publicly. I couldn't imagine what it would be like to have to talk about my spouse of twenty years from the pulpit less than three days after their death. Yet Pastor Tito stood before the congregation and gave a beautiful tribute to his life partner. Though I could tell he was in pain, he demonstrated an ease that could only come from a heart deeply rooted in Christ. His presentation concluded with a Word from Ecclesiastes by Pastor Tony and a video tribute. By the time the video was showing, I was sobbing as if I had just lost a dear friend I never knew. Romans 12:15 urges us to "Rejoice with those who rejoice; mourn with those who mourn" (NIV) and I couldn't help but empathize with Christian, who at ten years old would never see his biological mother again. Pastor Tony concluded the service with prayer, and I snuck away before the crowd of people could come out. I was not in the mood to have conversations with anyone. I was the first person leaving the lobby and Pastor Tito was already standing at the door to greet people. Don't say anything stupid I told myself when I saw him. I hugged him, uttered who knows what and walked out. I spent the rest of the morning laying on my couch and communicating with Specialist. Later that afternoon, my cell phone rang, and it was Pastor Tito.

"Hello," I answered, confused as to why he was calling me.

"Njiba, it's Pastor Tito. I am calling to check on you," he responded casually.

Taken aback by his words I answered, "Shouldn't I be the one checking on you? You just lost your wife?"

"Njiba, Traci went to be home with the Lord. Yes, I am grieving, but I am also still a pastor. I am still entrusted to care for God's people. You looked so broken when you left this morning and I made a mental note to reach out to you," he said with such poise.

I honestly thought he was crazy but went along with it.

"Thanks Pastor Tito. I appreciate it. You are usually jovial, and it was hard for me to watch you grieve. Plus, I kept thinking about Christian and Traci's mom. I mean I was just with everyone last month. It's still mind-blowing that Traci is gone."

"I can understand your sentiments Njiba. We have many people praying for us, and God's grace is sufficient," he confidently replied, and that was the end of that conversation.

Though I had to teach Monday, I spent the rest of Sunday in my own thoughts. I had seen Traci at church on multiple occasions, but never had a chance to know who she was. We exchanged the occasional church greetings, and I often complimented her outfit and hair. It seemed so unfortunate that she would be gone at such a young age. I had many unanswered questions and I believed I would have lived with the question marks had the Lord not orchestrated my relationship with Traci's best friend, Leia Hardimon. It was through the lenses of their relationship that I got to come close to knowing my husband's former wife, Traci Tirado.

How It Began by Leia Hardimon

As a new Christian at Hillcrest Church in 1999, I knew I needed to get involved, and I knew I loved working with kids. Tito was the Jr. High Pastor and I decided to start volunteering in that ministry. I remember interviewing with Pastor Tito and being terrified because I knew so very little about the Bible, faith, church… really everything—I was twenty-one. Pastor partnered me with his wife Traci for the sixth grade Sunday school class. Each week we were unpacking a foundation of faith. This was perfect for me because I needed to learn all these too! Traci was an excellent teacher. She had the kids memorizing Scripture, reading between lessons, even doing the homework! A month or so into the class she asked if I'd like to teach a lesson. I remember it was on the Trinity. I almost backed out a hundred times that week. How could someone that doesn't understand the Trinity teach it to sixth graders? Somehow, I survived that lesson and many after. One day, Traci asked if I could stay and talk for a few minutes. We sat on a staircase outside the classroom, and she literally said these words, "Will you be my friend?" It's comical looking back, but it seemed so perfect at the moment. She explained that being a pastor's wife she had difficulty making friends, but knew she really needed other women in her life. Awkward might be how you explain your answer to that question, but the result was yes… yes, I will be your friend.

Over the next years we dove into everything middle school ministry-related together. Bible studies, a drama team, small groups, camp and sleepovers filled our evenings and weekends. John began leading worship for some of the services and he and Tito became good friends. We were both young couples with no children yet—and we shared so many interests it was a perfect fit. From game nights to events, to lively political conversations, we enjoyed the kind of friendship that feels like family. Along the journey Traci and Tito wanted to start a family. Traci found that she would have to do in vitro in order to have a biological child. We had lunch one day and she was so very excited about carrying him this far and could feel him moving a bit. She had ideas for his room and couldn't wait to be a mom. A week later she lost him. We cried together. She and Tito made plans for him to be buried. It was so very important to her that the world recognize that Jireh was their first son.

Our love of God, our husbands, the youth, music, and art drew us together, but Traci and I were very different in one area. I am a planner. I like to have all the options laid out with all the scenarios thought through and then a period to think and process before any major changes. Even after that time period of thought I hate change and will avoid it at all cost. Traci made decisions on the spot (or at least it seemed). She had a confidence about her that she could look at two options, choose one and not look back. Once, she called me and said, "We are moving to New Mexico." I said, "When?" She answered, "Well… now… we are actually in the car right now." Now, I know there was probably a lot of prayer and consideration, but she and Tito often kept that private and so when they made up their minds and started running in a direction it sometimes caught me off guard.

While living in New Mexico Traci was still pursuing the in vitro and asked to come stay with us for four to six weeks. I was so very excited to have her come stay with us! I'd get to live with my best friend for weeks! The one downside was I would need to do her injections each day. I laugh looking back at the insane amount of hash browns I cooked for her when she was on bedrest, or the bags of white cheddar popcorn we devoured watching movies and how good I got at hormone injections!

Christian is the miracle that came from a miracle. Born at 1 pound, he was kept for months in the NICU and the Ronald McDonald House became home to Traci and Tito. There were months of thinking he wasn't going to make it. Months of diagnoses that were life threatening, life limiting and difficult. Obstacle after obstacle he fought and would prove them wrong. Traci told me about the calls they would get to come quick because he surely wouldn't make it through the night. They would pray, read Scripture, cry out in worship and God not only would spare his life, but He would make the impossible, possible. Christian is God's way of showing us that nothing is impossible for Him and prayers we don't even know to pray are answered. He will never sit up, he will never walk, he won't talk… the list of things we were all told Christian would never do goes on and on. Today he does all of these and more! He skates, he plays drums, he reads, he counts, he goes to school, he dresses and feeds himself, he plays piano and so much more. It has become a joke in our house, "What did they say he can't do now? Give him a couple months!" John and I are honored to be godparents of this amazing living reminder of God's love.

The Tirados moved back to Dallas, and we loved seeing them start a church. We were on staff elsewhere but would sneak over to worship with them as often as we could. Life got busier with us each having two kiddos and different churches and jobs, but somehow, we found ways to connect. Not as often as we wanted and certainly not the wealth of time we had before. Once Traci and I snuck away to a lunch and she asked why we weren't as close as before. I responded that we had four additional humans, and both were working a lot more AND we weren't at the same church so the natural life rhythm of church family wasn't there either. She said, "We choose to be busy, and we can control our schedules to make each other a priority." We both promised we would try more to prioritize our friendship. I've always felt bad that I wasn't always good at honoring that. I have lots of excuses, but the truth is… she's right—we choose busy and we can control a lot more than we think.

Pastor Tito was called to Virginia to minister, so once again our friendship became long distance. This time we made plans to each visit once a year and no shorter than 3 days. We agreed to find time weekly to talk on the phone and really tried to make our friendship a priority despite the distance. One day during our conversation, the tone of her voice was different. There was an urgency and a slight quiver. I sat in my hammock on my back patio, a common place I would go during our phone conversations. It was quiet and my kids would know mommy was "off duty" for a few minutes while on the phone with Aunt Traci. She proceeded to tell me that she had found a lump and had some tests run and it was breast cancer. We cried. We prayed. We talked for hours about options she'd researched. She clearly told me that she did NOT want to do traditional chemotherapy and radiation. She was not a vain person so don't read that into her decision. She didn't want to be made sick by poisons running through her veins. She didn't want to be cut up and pieced back together. She had researched and found other options and wanted to allow God to use His creation to heal her naturally. I did not know anything about the options she spoke of, but I knew she was solid in her plan of action and no use would come of arguing with her. The promise she made that night to me was that if the natural options were not working, she would change course and try traditional medicine. We talked about Christian and how she had to fight this in every possible way because he needed her. She said the strangest thing to me that night. "If I die you have to love whoever Tito marries." I blew her comment off, refusing to even think that far ahead and at that tragic of an outcome. I mean we just found out and we had a plan and she's the mightiest prayer warrior I've ever known. God was going to heal her and this would just be a chapter in her book.

We began talking more often, sharing information, keeping posted on how the treatments she was doing were going. Some made her very ill and very weak, but they worked, and the lump shrunk, so she stepped it up a notch and went on a very restrictive diet, exercise and lifestyle change plan. The designer of the program came and stayed with her for a time and taught her how to prepare food and how to maximize the impact of the plan. It worked; the tumor shrank again. Literally, she watched as the lump decreased from the size of a ping pong ball to the size of a pea. She was in tremendous shape at this time. All muscle, exercising, juicing, and eating all organic.

As a homeschool family we often work trips into our studies to bring a subject to life. Jamestown and Yorktown seemed like a perfect trip to bring American History to life, and it allowed me to sneak in several visits with Traci. She joined us on a tour or two and I turned a room of our condo into a slumber party—where we stayed up far too late talking and eating white cheddar popcorn. It was that night she told me the cancer was coming back and that she couldn't do the strict regimen anymore. She talked of how it isolated her from the world and made her unable to be involved in the lives of her husband and kids. It was just too difficult to maintain, and she didn't want to do it anymore. She said she was going to look at other options and see, but she was backing off the natural plans. In that visit she did not act as if she planned to give up or knew she could die. She simply wasn't going to go the natural route any longer. She seemed positive and confident as she shared plans to build a new house in a neighborhood, she'd been talking about for over a year. We toured a model home, and she explained every detail of how she had modified the plan for her family and what they needed. Everything seemed so normal.

A bit later that year she came for a visit to Dallas. Traci wanted to soak up life with me and our family. She had a new perspective it seemed. She was intentional about moments, savoring small things and wanting to experience all the things we talked about on the phone. Of all the things to do in Dallas she really wanted to go to the American Girl store. Samantha came to be her daughter after the age of all the bows, dolls and tea parties, and Traci wished she could have had those experiences with Sam. She often spoke of her love for Samantha and her wish to have had those moments with her. Upon her arrival in Dallas, we took her to lunch at the American Girl Cafe. We even loaned her a doll so she could fully participate in all the girly fun. We giggled, pretended, and spent the whole afternoon soaking in all the delights of the American Girl experience.

Traci had a dear friend that was fighting cancer as well and unfortunately was not doing very well. Traci asked me to take her to her house for a visit so she could pray with her and encourage her. She was so strong and such a perfect friend to this woman. Just a few weeks later the Lord allowed her body peace from the illness, and she passed. One afternoon we had a gymnastic meet for my daughter, Alexa. Traci asked dozens of questions, watched, cheered, and celebrated with us all day. I've taken lots of friends to gymnastics meets and about 2 hours in they are ready to go! Looking back, it was as if she was investing in Alexa in a way that would last forever. Later that weekend she went with Trinity to dance and watched her take African dance and Ballet class. Again, she asked questions, took it all in and had long discussions with Trinity about what dance meant to her. She was creating a connection with my girls that would plant roots of her love for them in their hearts. I don't know if she knew then or if she was just more deliberate about the importance of moments like this, but something eternal was bound that weekend in her relationship with my children.

The day she was scheduled to fly out she did the strangest thing. She woke up and insisted we find a Kinko's. I told her I'd made us lunch plans and we could find one right after that. We ate at a beautiful restaurant in Addison with a patio. The girls sandwiched her at the table. After lunch I took her to a Kinko's, and she wouldn't let me get out of the car. Apparently, that Kinko's did not have whatever it was that she needed so we went to another one and again I was told to wait in the car. After about 30 minutes she came out with an envelope and told me to open it. Inside were nearly a dozen photos she had taken of us over the week. Her insistence that she have those pictures printed before she left Dallas should maybe have caused suspicion, but Traci got ideas in her head all the time that had to happen, so I thought nothing of it. Looking back, I see this visit as her goodbye. She had treasured our time, lived it to the fullest and created memories that we treasure in our family. I wish I had known…

Spring passed quickly and with it was a very busy season with our family full of dance events and gymnastics meets. Traci seemed busy as well arranging programs for Christian and putting finishing touches on the new house. Somehow, our phone conversations became a bit more spread out and a text might not be returned for a few days. I never thought anything of it because when we did talk, she said she was feeling good. She was monitoring the growth and had seen her doctor. She had an appointment at the Cancer Center of America and asked me to go with her. I responded that I couldn't go because of some events my girls had, but they could conference me in and I'd be happy to help her navigate whatever they were recommending. Apparently, the visit did not go well because she didn't even call me until she got home. Perhaps it was just that the information she got was not what she wanted to hear. When we talked, she simply said, "They don't have a good plan for me because they won't help me unless I do chemotherapy, and I REFUSE to pump that poison into my body." She mentioned a surgeon that she'd been talking to that was looking to just remove the tumor, and she seemed hopeful about that. At this point she stopped offering information to me about her health. I had to draw it out of her and because of that change in her communication I thought she must be doing fine. She spoke of work, plans and the house. She talked about programs she'd found to help Christian and how her father-in-law was adjusting to his new diet. Her conversations seemed so alive, and her faith never wavered.

In late summer of 2015, she asked if I could come to her birthday. I couldn't because we already had something going on.

Something stupid, I'm sure. Something I could have moved or canceled or skipped, but instead I told her I'd be there around Christmas time. A bit later into the fall I texted her about a new preschool ministry position I had accepted. Her last text to me was her saying how perfect she thought I was for that and how awesome she knew I would do.

CHAPTER 9: THY WILL BE DONE

Florida Fling

November 2015 came with the beautiful embrace of fall and the leaves began to change. I have read somewhere that the only thing that remains constant in life is change and while growing up, this became my motto. I relinquished my ability to feel any sense of joy because I was so used to pain. This was a miserable existence, but I was still alive to call it my own. The changes came in different facets, but they all required proper adjustments. First, I had finally started my fall semester for the Educational Specialist program, and it was kicking my butt. I was struggling to manage a full-time job and maintain a 4.0 grade point average. Secondly, my relationship with Specialist seemed to have plateaued. We talked daily, we communicated well, and we chose to simply enjoy what was instead of thinking about what could be. Lastly, I was still attending Calvary, but I had not seen Pastor Tito for a few weeks. This was understandable given the circumstances.

Yet as the month of November began, Pastor Tito called me to ask what I was doing for Thanksgiving that year. I told him I did not have any concrete plans and was interested to know why he was calling. He shared with me that he and his family, which included Christian, his dad and their personal attendant, would be driving to Orlando, Florida to spend the holidays with Traci's mom. He mentioned how he was not fond of long-distance driving, but he knew I was. In addition, since I had been around them before, he could use the help on this twelve-hour trip. As a road trip lover, I immediately said sure without putting much thought to it. Interesting enough, LaShondra Rice, who by this point had become my godmother, was going to be in the United States from London. I casually shared with her Pastor Tito's proposal, and she said she needed to meet him before I could go. The second person I ran the trip by was Specialist. He did not have any reservations that I can recall since I had always expressed that Pastor Tito was like a big brother to me. Plus, it was a group trip to see his former in-laws. Kedra on the other hand, as excited as she was for me to get some fresh air, jokingly and seriously said to me, "Pastor or not, he is still a man Njiba."

Upon Mommy LaShondra's request, we had dinner at a Mexican restaurant so she could finally meet Pastor Tito. During our conversations, she expressed that she was thankful I had someone here who could biblically counsel me through the pain I had experienced during a failed engagement. She continuously mentioned how I was a fragile being who had experienced many traumatic events with no proper family support, but that God was working, and my years of rest would come. We briefly talked about me dating Specialist, which was news to Pastor Tito. Though we conversed in the lobby periodically, our relationship wasn't as such that I would come spill the beans about my intimate life. Thankfully, we switched the subject to him and where he saw himself relationally. Without hesitation, Pastor Tito said he would be married in a year or less. He expressed that he mourned his former wife during the last six months of her cancer, and they shared many conversations where she told him to find a good mom for Christian. In addition, he admitted that it was not good for him to be alone, and he would have to find a helpmeet for him. I was amazed by his confidence and how in tune he was with his own emotions. I secretly told myself that one day I hoped to be able to articulate how I feel and what I want with such an ease.

The following week while at church, Pastor Tito and a couple other members of the church took a picture together. As I was reviewing the picture, I jokingly said to Pastor Tito that he and the single woman next to him made a cute couple. He laughed and said he had attempted to talk to her, but she felt she had some type of allegiance towards Traci and could not entertain it. Pastor Tito conveyed relief in that news as he shared that he really did not want to date anyone in the church to begin with. This prompted me to ask him, "So exactly what are you looking for in a woman?" He gave me his qualifications, which didn't seem too demanding, and said he was going to try online dating. That afternoon, I specifically recall talking with Specialist about my conversation with Pastor Tito concerning the type of woman he was looking for in a wife. As soon as I finished my last word, Specialist exclaimed, "I know the woman he is describing." I rolled my eyes and pressed my ear to the phone to make sure I was hearing correctly. "And who exactly would that be?" I asked in an investigating tone. With all confidence he said, "YOU!" I immediately gasped for air. I told him that was disgusting, and I hoped he was joking. But he wasn't and conveniently dropped the subject.

On November 25th, 2015, around midnight I made myself comfortable in the driver's seat of Pastor Tito's car and began the journey to Orlando. The ride there was smooth. Pastor Tito rode in the passenger seat and we spent most of the time discussing the different women on Christian Mingle who were attempting to become the next Mrs. Tirado. Unfortunately for him, he confessed that he ended up doing biblical counseling on the phone with these women more than getting to know them for relationship purposes. Such were the disadvantages of being in ministry for over twenty years, married for twenty years and having to start over. With my limited wisdom, I chimed in where I could, and we had an enjoyable ride to Florida. We realized that we both enjoy working out and agreed to dedicate some of our time there going to the gym. Our arrival at Traci's mom's house midday brought many tears as her daughter had died a little more than a month ago. Seeing her grandchild brought so many emotions and pain, but being the woman of faith that she is, she was able to power through in between the tears. Pastor Tito showed me where I would be sleeping, and everyone retreated to relaxing. The next day was Thanksgiving and like most American families, Traci's mom was preparing the meals for the day. We decided to get in an early workout before indulging in all the food.

Thankfully, after trying several gyms, we found one that would give us guest passes without charging us anything. Pastor Tito and I went our separate ways to do our own workout routines. After a good sweat, we headed back to Traci's mom's house. In the car Pastor Tito kept talking about this one lady he had been texting with and even took out on a date. Though it seemed exciting, I saw no future in that relationship. So I casually told him he just needed to chill because she didn't seem like the woman that was fit for him. Then, there was an eerie silence in the car for the first time during our trip.

"You know what Njiba?" Pastor Tito finally broke the silence.

"What?"

He looked at me as he was driving and said, "If you weren't so young, I would date you."

I had to think of a comical comeback quick. I chuckled and sarcastically responded,

"If you weren't as old as Moses, I would date you too."

I couldn't believe I had said that. I was twenty-four and he was forty-seven. There was a huge age gap between us. I wasn't completely afraid of dating an older guy. I had done so before, but this was PASTOR TITO from my home church after all. Plus, he had just lost his wife. How could I possibly even entertain such a thought and respond pleasantly? Furthermore, Specialist was still in the picture despite how I felt about us. I laughed internally and chucked it off to another flirtatious conversation I had with a man.

When we got back to the house, we got busy in helping out and chose not to address the elephant in the room. I knew something had changed through those simple comments because we both started looking at each other through different lenses. I began to ask myself if I could see myself with a pastor, especially one from my own local church. I decided to fan these thoughts away. This is just a Florida Fling I told myself. That night, after all the festivities were over, we decided to address the elephant in the room. Pastor Tito began to ask me specific questions about my relationship with Specialist. I truly couldn't formulate many answers because I was not sure about how I felt concerning my relationship to him. I praised him for being such an awesome guy, and yet I thought to myself that maybe I was settling. Through a series of questions, we landed back to the hypothetical idea of Pastor Tito and I being a couple. We listed the pros and cons. I was so scared, but as someone who enjoyed the forbidden fruits life has to offer, I couldn't help but indulge in our "what if" scenario. I finally stopped myself when I started to wonder what my biological family would say. Pastor Tito was twenty-three years older than me; he had been married before and already had kids. Even if Samantha no longer lived at home, he took care of his father who also had medical demands. I had never envisioned myself taking on such responsibilities. In addition, I couldn't help but wonder how the people in the church would feel or what they would think. I mean, let's be honest. Traci had recently died, without allowing them the opportunity to truly grieve or be part of her diagnosis, and now, their beloved Associate Pastor wanted to bring someone new in the picture. I knew this was a recipe for disaster. I was getting tired with all these emotional conversations and my energy tank was depleted. We said goodnight and I went to sleep.

The next day, we worked out together again. I am not fond for making situations awkward and I love to alleviate any awkwardness with humor. This made for a smooth car ride and workout session. Afterwards, we found a smoothie place and enjoyed a few beverages outside with the Florida morning breeze hitting out faces. I wasn't sure if this would be considered a date, but it sure felt like it. We spent the rest of the day visiting Pastor Tito's side of the family. Since they were all from Puerto Rico, the main language of communication was Spanish. I didn't feel as lost because French is my first language, and I could make out things through context clues. One thing I did not need any clues for was how some of his family members were reacting to my presence. Though we weren't being love birds and I was spending most of my time with Christian, there was a perception that I may have been there for other reasons. I pretended I didn't feel the tension and kept it pushing.

Later that night, while talking with Pastor Tito, he expressed to me how he already knew what he wanted in a woman. He shared how he didn't have time to have a girlfriend and didn't like making things complicated. He then put the ball in my corner by saying he never thought he would choose someone who was twenty-three years younger. However, I had always demonstrated such maturity and strength that he wouldn't think twice. As I sat there with no words, he asked me to come closer. I slowly moved forward, and we kissed. I blinked hard and thought to myself, this only happens in movies. Then I thought about Specialist, and everything came crashing down. Internally, I started beating myself up. I should have never allowed myself to entertain my friendship with Specialist to the level it had gotten knowing that I didn't want to be with someone who lived so far away. I should have put boundaries in place like with other guys and been honest with myself. I should have said I was not interested instead of watering the possible seed called "us." But it was too late. I had strung him along and somehow; I would have to find a way to make this right. To appease the burden, I kept telling myself that the kiss with Pastor Tito did not mean anything. This was all a Florida Fling. We would drive back to Virginia the next day, and nothing would come of this.

I feel Safe

The drive from Orlando to Virginia felt like the shortest twelve hour drive I had ever taken. I was thrilled by the thought of being in my own apartment again and having a sense of normalcy. Amazingly enough, Pastor Tito and I rode back home holding hands the entire time. I must admit, it felt safe to be with him. I was afraid of what everyone would say and that I would wake up from this dream, but while it lasted, I enjoyed it. Upon our arrival to Newport News, I said goodbye to everyone casually and drove off. I just knew this would be it. I imagined how we would see each other at church on Sunday and give each other our typical greetings. Then, Pastor Tito asked if he could take me to lunch after church. That's when I realized this wasn't a dream. That night I contacted Specialist and simply told him I needed a week to settle things in my heart and mind. He had already been sensing me being distant prior to my Florida trip after I confessed that I hadn't given my best yes. Being the amazing and understandable person that he is, he told me that was fine. He would miss me terribly, however.

During my lunch date, I couldn't believe I was out with Pastor Tito. I kept looking at him and saying, "But you're Pastor Tito!" To which he would respond, "And you're the girl from the Welcome Center." Over our meal, he expressed again his sentiments towards "us" and spoke so highly over me. I had never seen or been with a man whose emotional intelligence and expression literally took my breath away. I seriously had to ask him to stop talking more than once so I could catch my breath. I listened to him, afraid of all the many unknowns. I had done some crazy things before but moving forward with him would be permanent. I wouldn't be agreeing to simply date him. I would be agreeing to being his wife. Like a gentleman, he told me it was my decision and either way he would respect it. From the time I was in his presence, he opened my doors, pulled out my chairs, helped with my coat and of course, paid for everything. I had been on dates with guys who attempted to impress me, but Tito as I could now call him was on a different level. At the end of our date, I asked him if I could have a week to think things through. Like Specialist, he insisted that it would be hard to not communicate with me, but he would respect my wishes. I had every intention to not speak to either Pastor Tito or Specialist so that I could really pray and think more clearly. Unfortunately, I failed miserably with staying disconnected from Pastor Tito via phone, and every time it was me initiating! I couldn't believe I was being that girl. Of course, he didn't mind my initiated communication and we have talked every day since.

After the weekend, I had to make one of the hardest calls ever. I realized I couldn't continue to let Specialist think we had a future to build when I couldn't see it. On paper he was a great match and fit quite well. Yet somehow, I had a hunch that being with him wasn't it.

He did not take the news too well at all. He acknowledged the fact that I was honest along the journey concerning being in a long-distance relationship again. He admitted that he really fell for me and was on a quest to convince me otherwise by making this work. I knew he was upset, and I truly felt the heaviness of his heart through the phone. We said our goodbyes, but I knew it wouldn't be the end of our conversation. I knew we would have subsequent conversations via text message as both of us processed what was, what could have been and what is. After that conversation with Specialist, I went to see Pastor Tito face-to-face for the first time since our date Sunday. The entire family was home including the attendant and I thought to myself, this could be my reality. How would we ever get any alone time? We sat at the dining room table, and I couldn't even look at him in his eyes.

"After much thought and consideration," I finally started. "I honestly don't know what the best answer here is. Nevertheless, I can't tell you where we are going, and I didn't get any confirmation from God that I am supposed to marry you. What I do know though is, I FEEL SAFE WITH YOU," and cue sigh of relief. Pastor Tito looked at me with a confused regard and asked me what that meant. I had no proficient answer. He understood and took what I said for what it was worth. I was there with him. It was December 4th, 2015.

From Pastor to Amor

Aside from accepting the person, principles, and practices of Jesus Christ, whom you choose as a life partner is the most consequential decision you will ever make. Marriage is honorable and ordained by God. Saying "I do" to someone means more than just getting a person. In saying "I do," you aren't just getting a companion. Saying "I do" on your wedding day indicates that you are getting a partner who will contribute to the course and quality of your life. Though I did not know that God had prepared me to be Pastor Tito's helpmeet, I knew walking this journey of feeling safe with him meant being married to him in the long run. We celebrated Christmas 2015 and brought in the New Year together while attempting to keep our relationship discreet. Being in leadership and the man that continuously aims to live above reproach, Tito immediately told Pastor Tony, who like everyone had his reservations. I went ahead and told Mommy LaShondra and Daddy Edwin, who also had reservations. For both parties, the reservations did not come only from the age gap, but also from the fact that Traci had only been dead for less than three months. "Take your time" was the common phrase.

Knowing we would face many opposing views, we started praying daily in the morning and at night over the phone. We decided to start fasting every Thursday and make our relationship a matter of prayer. We knew what we were embarking on was nothing conventional nor did it make sense to anyone. Shoot, it didn't make sense to me either. I was continuously in prayer and felt as though I wasn't getting a concrete answer. On February 19, 2016, during a Spirit & Truth prayer night, I found myself at the altar. I was sobbing and weeping. I felt the heaviness of walking in this journey of ever becoming Mrs. Tirado. I prayed earnestly that night. I felt like Jesus in Luke 22:42 saying, "Father, if you are willing, take this cup from me; yet not my will, but yours be done" (NIV). Except in my cries to the Lord, I asked Him for a distinctive sign that I was walking on the right path. I told Him I couldn't and wouldn't be able to see this through on my own. That night I went to sleep in expectancy. The Lord has often revealed Himself to me in dreams. Though at a young age I wanted to shut off that part of my makeup, I had learned to embrace it. During my dream that night, I saw myself going over to my adoptive parents' house and telling them all about Tito. In my dream, both were very excited for me. I was shocked by their response because it was not their norm. The Holy Spirit whispered slowly, "Do not be afraid. I am with you." I woke up that morning and immediately uttered, "Oh my gosh! I am supposed to marry him."

I called my adoptive dad that morning and told him I would stop by the house to see him. During my visit, I told him there was a man who was interested in marrying me. I told him his age, his past, his profession and how many children he had. For the very first time I was straightforward, honest, and unapologetically bold. My adoptive father immediately began to thank God and had the same reaction as the one from my dream. Later that evening, we picked up my adoptive mom from work and I took them out to dinner. As I shared the news with her, she was not as enthused as my adoptive father, but she said she was happy for me. They both asked when Tito planned to come over to present himself with his family or closest friends who could serve as witness. Being that I had already explained to Tito how things ran in the African abode, he casually mentioned, what about March 12th? My eyes opened wide in disbelief, but he was serious. I told my adoptive parents the 12th and the date seemed to work for everyone.

We gathered at my adoptive parents' house on March 12th. A few of my adoptive siblings and Naomi were there. Tito brought his best friend and another pastor friend to be his witnesses given that his family members are not in Virginia. During the presentation, he asked for my hand in marriage and expressed the timeline in which we would both like for it to happen. We had a plan in place. Since Tito already had a house and I had an apartment with a lease ending in May, we saw no advantage in keeping the apartment for another year. Tito and I had agreed that we would do the dowry in June of 2016 and do the religious ceremony in 2017. Tito was frank with my adoptive parents about not being able to live under the same roof unless we had an official document to prove our marriage. My adoptive father, being the man of tradition, insisted that his only cultural requirement was the dowry. To which Tito explained that we would more than likely be married by the time we came to the house for the dowry to ensure we fulfilled both the law and the culture. We ate and celebrated. Everyone left with a clear understanding of our timeline.

Remember when I prayed, asking God that I wouldn't have to have a long courtship with the man I was to marry? Well, the Lord sure does have a sense of humor. He gave me a man who only had two speeds: fast and very fast! After the presentation on March 12th, Tito proposed on March 18th, and we were legally married on April 1st.

Things were moving and had moved so fast, it felt like a roller coaster with no end. Everything in me wanted to shut down and run away. Being in my first healthy, honest, godly relationship was scary. It challenged all the toxic and dysfunctional behaviors I had internalized over the years. By being with Tito, saying "I feel safe" was no longer good enough. It's easy to give someone your body. It's harder to give someone your heart, especially if your heart has been shattered multiple times and there are parts of you that you dare not to share again. But Tito challenged me to dig deeper within myself and express the raw emotions I was feeling. Not only did he challenge me to identify them, but he also asked me to question why I was feeling this way. Together we read books on healing as I shared with him my past with the rape and promiscuity, which eventually lead to forgiveness. He covered me in prayer daily and washed me with God's Word. He pointed me to Christ. He believed in my goals enough to suggest I take time off work to focus on school and take other things off my plate. Looking back, I can see his wisdom in many ways but there were so many moving parts all taking place at the same time.

I wish I could say that pain stopped befriending me on April 1st, 2016, as I committed my life to my husband. There were a series of events that happened leading up to us getting married and from that day on. I will spare the details in this book because marriage, family fallouts, church hurt, and parenting all deserve their own pages to fully convey what it meant for me to adjust from one hat to another. The truth of the matter nonetheless is, there were many painful moments in my twenty-five-year journey leading up to becoming Tito's wife. Some inflicted by others and some caused by me to myself or to others. Yet when I reflect, I can see how each year in the desert since my biological parents' death had been worth this promised land. My promised land has meant walking in complete obedience to God's Word. My promised land has meant living in the freedom of God's grace. My promised land has meant walking in wholeness despite my deepest wounds. Not because I chose to pretend that past or present painful actions didn't impact me. I simply fully recognized that *God has changed the meaning of the pain by weaving it in the design and purpose of my life, so that it lies in the power of His redeeming love.*

December 21, 2015

Hi Abuser.

I am sure this message comes to you in surprise. First and foremost, I pray that you are well, as well as your daughter. Interesting enough, I wondered what I would ever say to you if I ever crossed paths with you again. For many years, the thought of you angered me and brought much pain to my heart. You took something so precious away from me at such a young age that left me with scars that I will live with forever as a reminder of my story and testimony. But I thank God that Christ didn't remove the memory, but simply He removed the pain associated with that memory. I could ask you many questions as to why this or that? Or what were you thinking? But I have learned that God does not change the actual, factual nature of evil that occurs. Humanly speaking, nothing can change this; it's still evil, tragic, senseless, and perhaps unjust and absurd. But God can change the meaning of it for our total lives. God can weave it into the design and purpose of our lives, so that it lies within the circle of His redeeming and recycling activity. With that in mind, I felt compelled to let you that I have forgiven you for what you did, and I pray that you may find healing in knowing so. Take care of yourself and I wish you nothing but the best.

******

Hello Laura,

You are right that your message came as a great surprise, it surely was the last thing I expected, but something I needed the most. I recall writing a letter back in 2003 during the separation as I was asking for forgiveness to everyone, but I don't think I ever asked one from you. To which I'm taking the first opportunity now even though it has already been mentioned in your letter: I hope you could find in you the opportunity to forgive my selfish acts that may have affected you in countless ways that I wouldn't dare enumerate at the moment, and mostly that the world with all its magnificent resources could help you recover from those dreadful experiences. I had a very hard time replying to your message because there is so much that I wanted to say but cannot find the appropriate words to illustrate my thoughts. You have no idea how much it means to read something like this especially coming from you. There isn't a moment that goes by that I am not reminded of the evil deeds that occurred that year and a little before then. I have struggled with this throughout High School and mainly college. I remember attending counseling which advised me to come forth and ask you personally for forgiveness, which I tried to do via social media at the time, but I am assuming the timing, nor my approach was right, and honestly, I did not know how to handle it properly. I am reminded of these shameful acts of mine every time I raise my head and try to forget things. I can honestly tell you that also everything I read takes me back to those years, and there is at least one question asked to me in most conversation that has to remind me of all of this, to the point that I felt no different than the savages that are committing atrocities against women in the eastern part of our country, or the thugs on our streets. And I would even try to imagine what you were going through and that's what hurts me the most Laura. Not the fact that I must bear the constant pounding of the horrific memories, but that you could be going through the same thing if not much worse. I know you mentioned your thoughts as to what you would say to me if you saw me, those thoughts came across my mind too, and I can honestly say I tried my best to avoid that from happening. Not because I was afraid of the hatred that could have been lacerated at my person but rather the fact that I would reopen this big wound that has yet to start properly healing. I am glad that you found it in you not just to forgive me but to let me know in writing, I know it must have been very hard on your part, but it means a lot that it came from you and no one else. You seem to have found the peace through religion and Christ and I hope that guidance will continue to enlighten you through all your endeavors. I'm personally not much of an active religious person but also pray for all of us, knowing that things may never go back to normal but hope the best for the future. Your letter started with such kind words for me and my little girl; it really took me by surprise. I didn't know you were aware of her existence, Thank you. She is doing well. I sporadically hear a lot of great things about your progress and hope life continues to treat you very well as you have always been a smart hard-working person. All the best to you and the entire family out there. My apologies, _____.

Dear ___________,

What a heartfelt message. I can tell that you poured your heart out and were genuine in it. I am proud of you. I am praying for you and hope that today is the beginning of your walk-in freedom! I can't say we didn't share the same experience. I didn't go as far as counseling, but I had to examine certain things in my life that often took me back to those experiences and I thank God for some amazing people He put in my life to help through this journey. As I mentioned before, it's part of our story but I thank God that the book didn't end there. I pray that starting today you can have the memory but not the pain associated with it. Your daughter is beautiful. I have seen her in pictures. God has blessed you with the gift of fatherhood. Love her unconditionally. Show her what it means to be treated by a man. Protect her and live out a life that will be an example to her. Sometimes we don't get a chance to go back in history and rewrite the story, but God blesses us with new beginnings. New opportunities to do it right. I pray that God's grace will carry you through this journey and that when you wake up tomorrow, you can bask in God's mercies, love, and peace. I don't know what the future holds either because God has a way of handling our lives in ways that only He knows. But one thing I know for sure, your apology is accepted!

God bless, Laura

CHAPTER 10: P.U.R.P.O.S.E.

When facing painful encounters, it is almost impossible to see the light at the end of the tunnel because oftentimes we truly walk by sight and not by faith. We tend to be more in tune with our natural realities and truths based on our five senses. Yet our ability to find purpose in our pain can only come with a shift in perspective. No matter how difficult or trying our circumstances may be, God is in the business of reversing the irreversible to make His name known. This however cannot happen if we think with our own understanding. If you want to experience the supernatural in any crisis that you are facing in the natural, you must bring the divine perspective into your human reality. In Isaiah 55 verses 8 and 9, God declares these words, "For My thoughts are not your thoughts, nor are your ways My ways. For as the heavens are higher than the earth, so are My ways higher than your ways, and My thoughts than your thoughts" (NJKV). Therefore, inviting the divine perspective into our realities entails our diligence in knowing who God is through His Word and a continuously growing relationship with Jesus Christ. As I began to write this book, the Holy Spirit brought to my mind the word *purpose*. I have heard this word used more times than I want to recount. Each time, it has been defined in a way to fit the context of the writer. God being all knowing, knows my apprehension towards this word, yet it kept coming back to my spirit. Eventually, I prayed and asked the Lord to reveal to me how finding purpose in pain was relevant to this book and how exactly should I define it? One early morning as I lay in bed, a still small voice, almost like a whisper, directed me towards what I have come to embrace as the meaning of P.U.R.P.O.S.E. Through this acronym, I have found that every pain worked out for my good, to bring God glory and to help me minister to others. So, think back to whatever painful encounter(s) you thought about when you began reading my story and I pray that the next few pages will be a catalyst to empower you to walk victoriously.

Peace

One of the greatest lessons I learned from Pastor Tony at Calvary was that "There is nothing that happened in my life that had not been filtered through God's love." Now if I must be honest, losing both of my parents did not seem like something a loving God would allow. However, one of the first things I had to do in my journey of healing was to make peace. Merriam Webster defines peace as "a state of tranquility or quiet; freedom from disquieting or oppressing thoughts or emotions; harmony in personal relations" and sadly, it is very difficult for any human to live in a constant state of peace that is willed by our own flesh. The peace we offer ourselves through our human realities is temporary, short-lived, and often dependent on something or someone else. Yet through Scripture, our Creator demonstrates that we can be at peace with God and have the peace of God.

In Romans 5 verses 1 through 2, the Apostle Paul explains our position as Christians and our standing with Christ saying, "Therefore, having been justified by faith, we have peace with God through our Lord Jesus Christ, through whom also we have access by faith into this grace in which we stand, and rejoice in hope of the glory of God" (NKJV). In other words, our connection to the Father is solid, constant and rooted in Christ. Therefore, the beginning of finding purpose in our pain is by being in right relationship with God, through Christ. Romans 8:5–8 says,

> For those who live according to the flesh set their minds on the things of the flesh, but those *who live* according to the Spirit, the things of the Spirit. [6] For to be carnally minded *is* death, but to be spiritually minded *is* life and peace. [7] Because the carnal mind *is* enmity against God; for it is not subject to the law of God, nor indeed can be. [8] So then, those who are in the flesh cannot please God. (NKJV)

With many trials already in my repertoire by the age of fourteen, I remember vividly walking to the altar in 2005 to make Christ my personal Savior and welcoming the Holy Spirit to live inside me. This was the beginning of me being in right standing with God by faith in a positional manner, which then allowed me not only to be God's creature made in His image, but now an heir as the daughter of the King. Being at peace with God removed the shame of the scarlet letter S, sin, which I had been carrying. Through the work of Jesus, I understood that my debt was paid in full at the cross.

Secondly, not only should we have peace with God, but we should also experience the peace of God. Knowing that He would not be with them long, in John 14:27 Jesus tells His disciples, "Peace I leave with you; my peace I give you. I do not give to you as the world gives. Do not let your hearts be troubled and do not be afraid" (NIV). Sometimes as believers our hearts are calm despite the circumstances we face and other times, it feels like an ocean is churning inside us. This is to be expected as we live in a world where evil exists, or we simply make wrong decisions. Nevertheless, we can access the peace of God. Scripture tells us in Philippians 4:6–7, "Be anxious for nothing, but in everything by prayer and supplication, with thanksgiving, let your requests be made known to God; and the peace of God, which surpasses all understanding, will guard your hearts and minds through Christ Jesus" (NKJV). Experiencing the peace of God requires us to be people of prayer and thanksgiving. God's promise to us is that in doing so, He would provide us with peace that surpasses all understanding. Again, it's this concept Jesus talked about when He told His disciples that His peace was not like the world's peace. God's peace is a divine intervention in the midst of crisis. It gives us the ability to come face-to-face with the reality of our pain, yet supernaturally embrace God's sovereignty and love.

Though I had made peace with God, it took me a long time to walk in the freedom found at the cross of Christ. If I could do it all over, I would have surrendered my heart fully to Him and walked in obedience to His Word sooner. But my times are in His hands and therefore, I not only made peace with God, but I also made peace with all the things that happened to me as a child that I couldn't control. It doesn't mean I had to like it or be in agreement with it. It just means that through the renewing of my mind, I acknowledge that those events were evil, tragic, senseless, perhaps unjust and absurd. And at the same time, God was good, still is good and will always be good. With this in mind, I can be grateful for the vessels that were used to bring me to the United States, even if the means to the end wasn't exactly how I wish it would have been.

REFLECTION

1. Have you made peace with God?

---

2. Are you experiencing the peace of God?

Understanding

Proverbs 9:10 reads, "The fear of the LORD *is* the beginning of wisdom, and the knowledge of the Holy One is understanding" (NKJV). As a new believer reading the Bible and finding it quite boring, I was amazed by how the Bible tells us to fear God. In my dysfunctional understanding of relationships, I knew I didn't want to serve God if He required me to fear Him. I equated my relationship to God to my paternal uncles and their wives who mistreated me and out of fear I attempted to "behave" adequately. But as I grew in the Lord, I realized that fearing God was more out of reverence and love for Him. In reverencing Him, I was at the beginning stages of gaining wisdom and understanding.

When Adam and Even lived in the Garden of Eden the Lord told them they could enjoy all things abundantly except for touching the tree. Through the deceptive power of Satan, Eve was deceived, and Adam disobeyed God's orders. Through their disobedience, the Scriptures tell us that sin entered the world and became a fallen place. Understanding this has been crucial in my processing of pain because it gave me new clarity on who I am. Romans 3:10 says, "As it is written: there is none righteous, no, not one," and 1 John 1:8 reads, "If we say that we have no sin, we deceive ourselves, and the truth is not in us" (NKJV). These two verses allowed me to see that I was no different from the people who had wronged me. Even when I professed to be a Christian, I did not become sinless. I have hurt people along the way with lies, deceit, manipulation, and pride.

As I looked at my own list of transgressions, I understood that Christ had forgiven me of so much. Therefore, while I could acknowledge the wrongs or evil of others, I understood that it wouldn't be wise to live life as a victim: "For as by one man's disobedience many were made sinners, so also by one Man's obedience many will be made righteous" (Romans 5:19, NKJV). My reverence of God and understanding of man's fall enabled me to write a letter to my abuser and tell him he was forgiven. I had admitted to myself that I had forgiven him but hearing his name would make my skin crawl. It wasn't until I sought out the wisdom of God, not to understand why things happened to me, but more so why did things happen for me, that I felt the Holy Spirit prompting me to release my abuser and wish him well. On December 21st, 2015, as I wrote to him on Facebook, the words came with ease because they were spirit led. I was able to empathize with my abuser's sin nature and forgive him, others, and myself because I finally understood my sins were no different. Apart from Christ, I was separated from God and heading to hell, eternally unable to be reconciled to God. Fearing God and growing in the knowledge of the Holy One gave birth to my ability to process pain in a manner that was beyond simply singing, "Woe is me."

REFLECTION

1. Are there people in your life whom you need to forgive? If you have already forgiven them, do they know?

____

____

____

2. Have you reflected on the magnitude of your own sinfulness and empathized with those who have wronged you?

____

____

____

Restoration

Restoring is defined by Merriam Webster as, "to put or to bring back into existence or use." When restoration occurs, there must be work done. The beautiful part of God is that He is a God who loves a good comeback plot just like all of us. I recently watched my favorite college football team Alabama defeat Georgia after being down by fourteen points for most of the game. The quarterback Jalen Hurts, who had not played for most of the season due to injuries came in during the fourth quarter to replace the starting quarter back. The strange thing about watching this happen is the fact that Jalen had to be replaced last season by the now starting quarterback, Tua Tagovailoa. The suspense was high, and Alabama's win made for a great comeback story.

Another story I love is the story of Joseph in Genesis because it is a story of restoration. After being sold by his brothers, Joseph goes through a series of trials and tribulations. Yet at the end of the story, we see that God uses what was meant for evil to save not only Joseph and his family, but nations. What is fascinating is not just what God did, but also how Joseph participated in the process. He was diligent in doing his work while at the palace. He was faithful to God and was a trustworthy person. Upon being established as leader and having the opportunity to dwell in unforgiveness towards his brothers, Joseph chose to restore his relationship with his brothers as they demonstrated a heart of repentance. Unfortunately, many people believe that forgiveness and restoration of relationship are the same thing. When resolving conflict, it is imperative to know that God calls us to confront the person and their fault privately (Matthew 18). If they listen, you have won them over. If not, you are called to bring a witness. If they don't listen with the witness, then you are called to bring the matter to the church.

God in his infinite wisdom knew that we as fleshly human beings would have conflict. In John 16:33 Jesus tells us that in this world we will have trouble and at the same time, in Matthew 18, He gives us steps by which if it is possible on our part, to live at peace with everyone (Romans 12:18). While living at peace with everyone may not always be attainable even when you do try, God has a way of restoring the pieces of our lives that are broken and filling the voids we carry when we entrust ourselves to Him. After many years of crying about the death of my parents and wishing I had functional relationships with those who took care of me afterwards, the Lord was true to His word from Joel 2:25, which says, "So I will restore to you the years that the swarming locust has eaten" (NKJV). He placed LaShondra and Edwin Rice in my life at a moment when I needed much prayer, love, and support that could only come from a parental unit. Though they are not my biological parents, their existence in my life has given me a glimpse of what could have been had David and Nadine Kasonga stayed alive for the long haul. From long hours on the phone, to walking me down the aisle, to being in the delivery room when Tito Kaden was born, Mommy and Daddy Rice have been exceedingly above all that I could imagine.

Furthermore, through a series of Google searches, I was able to reconnect to a maternal uncle of mine who gave me many of Maman's family contact information. Through these relationships, I have been able to get a better understanding of who Maman was and feel forever connected to her. In addition, though all my siblings have not been in the same room since 2002, with the advancement of technology and social media, we have all been able to stay in touch and build a rapport that is healthy. My oldest sister Suzanne and I have had a strenuous relationship since we were younger. As she came to the United States in 2006, the only thing we truly shared was DNA. Yet with time, I have learned and grown to know her as a person, her likes, dislikes, joys, and struggles. This took over ten years of continual attempt to bond and communicating openly. Through our common love for Christ, we have come to spend hours on the phone reminiscing on our childhood and seeing how seeds of jealousy, betrayal and comparison were planted early on to expedite our disapproval of one another. We laugh and rejoice at our victories, but also know there is still much work to be done. Naomi, on the other hand, has blossomed before my eyes and we share a special bond that cannot be broken. Throughout the book, I refrained from sharing many of my siblings' personal stories because I believe it is not my place to do so and I hope one day they will each tell their stories through whatever means they want. But I am so thankful to no longer feel the emptiness of having a family whom I only feel connected to by DNA. Furthermore, I have forgiven my violator. I have also chosen to forgive the things I deemed were wrongly done to me by my adoptive parents or any relatives who took us under their wings after Papa and Maman died. I have also asked to be forgiven when given the opportunity, whether others acknowledge their wrongs or not. In the same token, I have learned to do relationship with boundaries.

Not only did I gain restoration with my siblings and maternal side of the family, but the Lord allowed me to foster relationships within my church community and circle of friends that have become a central core to my existence. Many of these people are believers in Christ and some aren't. However, my heart's participation in the restoration process stemmed not only from choosing to forgive those who wronged me, but also choosing to believe the best in others without being naïve. As a girl who really disliked having female friends, the Lord brought a plethora of women whom I could "show myself friendly" (Proverb 18:24, NKJV) with. Some of those friendships were seasonal, while others have been long-lasting. No matter the duration, each woman chipped away at the cemented bricks that protected my heart. I also became diligent in asking others to forgive me for my wrongs. Recognizing my own pride and sinful nature, confessing it to God and asking Him to mold me into who He wants me to be, which is Christ-like, has led me to do relationships in a way that honors Him.

There may be a situation or people in your life you are dealing with where you see no hope. Remember Scripture urges us to live at peace with everyone. This doesn't mean everyone will be your best friend, that you must agree with their thoughts, beliefs or even endorse their sins. Nonetheless, God is still in the restoration business. He can turn things around even when it looks like you have lost time, strength and opportunity. But your heart needs to be willing to participate in trusting God in the process. Notice I didn't say, your heart needs to feel like participating. Sometimes when you act in faith without feeling the faith, God will honor your obedience and increase your faith. Do what Jesus tells you to do even if you don't feel that it will work based on your education, expertise, history or whatever else you can think of. God is saying, "Behold, I am doing a new thing; now it springs forth, do you not perceive it? I will make a way in the wilderness and rivers in the desert" (Isaiah 43:19, ESV). Will you trust Him on the journey

REFLECTION

1. What areas in your life need restoring?

___

___

___

2. Who are the people in your life you need to ask to forgive you?

___

___

___

3. What have you done to be a participant in your restoration process?

___

___

___

Patience

In 1 Samuel 1 we are introduced to the family of Elkanah, who was married to Hannah. Hannah did not have children because as verse 6 tells us, "The Lord had closed her womb." Elkanah's second wife, Penninah, had children and would provoke Hannah severely. Each year Hannah would go to the house of the Lord having been provoked and weep without eating. Can you imagine the pain Hannah must have been feeling? Her desire was to have children, but she was physically incapable and on top of that, she had a rival in her face ready to remind her of her infertility. I don't know if you know anyone who struggles or has struggled with infertility, but most have a hard time even articulating the pain and grief they experience on the journey. It is a pain that is often hard to comfort. Even Elkanah tells his wife in verse 8, "Hannah, why do you weep? Why do you not eat? And why is your heart grieved? Am I not better to you than ten sons?" Without any response, the text tells us that Hannah rose and goes to pray. I loved how raw and real the Bible gets with this story. Hannah doesn't pretend that she is not experiencing frustration in this waiting period. "She was in bitterness of soul, and prayed to the Lord and wept in anguish" (verse 10). When was the last time you were honest with God about your frustrations and situation? The good news for all of us is that God is not intimated by our emotions. He created us in His image and knew us in our mother's womb. Though one of the fruits of the Spirit is self-control, by no means should we be hypocritical with God. After all He is all knowing.

Then Hannah does something drastic. Maybe it was an act of desperation or faith, but she cries out to God with a conditional statement. I don't know about you, but I have found myself in those moments where I saw no outs and started praying, God if you______ then I will__________. And boy has God been faithful even when I have been faithless and disloyal. Hannah prays in verse 11,

> O Lord of hosts, if You will indeed look on the affliction of Your maidservant and remember me, and not forget Your maidservant, but will give Your maidservant a male child, then I will give him to the Lord all the days of his life, no razor shall come upon his head. (NKJV)

Talk about a bold prayer! After much waiting, Hannah pleads with God to remember her and presents herself humbly as His maidservant. I am sure she had prayed many prayers prior to this one. Yet this specific prayer was different because it came with a condition. Sometimes God will keep us in a place that looks like it isn't going anywhere because He is after something bigger than just answering our prayers. Through Hannah came the Prophet Samuel, who anointed the first king of Israel, Saul. God can keep us in an extended waiting place for a deeper purpose.

During my dating days, the Lord brought some men in my path whom I truly thought would be my husband. Each relationship failed to work, or I would simply feel that it wasn't in my best interest to proceed. I now realize though I had a desire to be married, God was after something bigger. He was after my heart, my worship and intimacy with Him. And while being impatient, I entangled myself in relationships I shouldn't have been in. All this because I wasn't trusting in God's perfect timing. God was working on me and those around me so that I could eventually become the bride He has called me to be. To steward and process our pain in a way that honors God, we must learn to be patient with others, ourselves and God. I love defining patience as waiting with a joyful heart because my joy is not dependent on my circumstances. My joy is dependent on the God I serve. Through His Word, I have learned that He is a promise keeper. Psalm 40:1 says, "I waited patiently for the Lord; and He inclined me, and heard my cry" (NKJV).

Our pain can tend to keep us trapped in yesterday, ruining today and leaving us hopeless for tomorrow. So, what do we do while we wait? We must be people who praise and pray. In her prayer, Hannah begins by acknowledging that God is the Lord of hosts. He is above all. Then she proceeds to making her requests known to God. It is imperative that we praise God during our pain and not necessarily because of it. In magnifying God, the smaller that which is keeping us hostage becomes. This is not because our pain has changed in size, but because God is bigger in our sight. Secondly, there must be prayer as we are going through the pain. You must remind yourself that prayer gives us perspective, confidence and protection, and releases grace. Not only should we pray, but we should get other believers to pray with us because "The effectual fervent prayer of a righteous man availeth much" (James 5:16, KJV). Oftentimes we don't want others to know "our business" and yes, we must use wisdom. However, God did not intend for us to do life alone. Therefore, it is imperative that even in our moments of weakness and awaiting healing, that we come alongside others because God may just send our healing through others.

REFLECTION

1. What are you still waiting to see God do in your life?

____
____
____

2. How can you praise God amid your pain?

____
____
____

3. Who are the people God has sent your way to help you see His redeeming love, redemption, restoration and healing?

____
____
____

Opportunity

I remember sitting outside at CNU one year with a young lady who was a freshman. She had just had an argument with a guy she liked and some of the words that were exchanged in the argument took her back to some painful events in her past. I remember listening to her and truly understanding every emotion and thought she was feeling. As we sat under the night sky, I was able to comfort, encourage and uplift her. After praying with her, I remember walking to my room and saying out loud, "God I now see why I had to go through that." It was the very first time I was grateful for the pain I had endured. I would never want to relive it, but in that moment, I realized my healing was bigger than me. It was orchestrated so that I would have opportunity. Not just opportunities to tell my story, but opportunities to minister to others in a way that glorifies Christ.

In Matthew chapter 4 when Jesus is recruiting His disciples, He finds Peter fishing and tells him to follow Him as He would make him a fisher of men. Later in John chapter 21, after His resurrection, Jesus finds Peter fishing again. Peter had denied Jesus three times after he "grossly overestimated his strength and underestimated his weakness" (Dr. Tito Tirado). After attempting to catch some fish and having no success, Jesus shows up on the scene. He tells them to cast their net on the right side of the boat and they will catch some. If I was Peter, who had been in the business of fishing for a long time, I probably would have had an objection. Nonetheless, the men cast their net and they catch exceedingly more than they could have imagined. After they share a meal, Jesus reinstates Peter by telling him, "Feed my lambs, take care of my sheep, feed my sheep" (John 21:15–17, NKJV). This is an important moment in Peter's journey. He is once again being commissioned to be a fisher of men because Psalm 100:3 tells us to "Know that the LORD is God. It is He who made us, and we are His; we are His people, the sheep of His pasture" (NIV).

Processing our pain in a way that honors God allows us to see that we are ministers with a ministry out of our misery. When we entrust our pain to God, we become vessels of hope in the midst of despair and a fallen world. Through our relationship with Him, God allows us to heal, be blessed and help others on their journey. We can triumph over the schemes of Satan by the blood of the lamb and by the word of our testimony. I used to be so afraid of people knowing what happened to me. For the longest time fear had a grip on me. I was scared about what people would say or think. I was scared about how my biological family would feel about me having "our business" out in the open. Then one day I read that "God has not given us a spirit of fear, but of power and of love and of a sound mind" (2 Timothy 1:7, NKJV) and everything clicked for me. "The Son of Man has come to save and seek that which was lost" (Luke 10:19, NKJV), and until I surrendered by my life to Christ, I was lost. Given the trials and tribulations I endured, I could have been dead after attempting suicide twice. I could have been on medication for anxiety and depression. I could have been seeing counselor after counselor. But I have not. By his stripes, I have been healed (Isaiah 53:5, NKJV).

I have nothing against medication and counseling. Yet I realized God healed me in a unique way so that I could discover that the irreversible can be made reversible by an all-powerful God to bring about my comeback. The existence of Njiba is not my story. It has been His story all along. I have just been privileged with the opportunity to steward this journey, "For it has been granted to you on behalf of Christ not only to believe in Him, but also to suffer for Him" (Philippians 1:29, NIV) and ultimately win souls for the kingdom. The same is true for you. Don't underestimate the power of your journey or your pain. No matter how big or small it may be, God wants to use it for your greatest good and His glory. There are people and places that are meant to be impacted through you. Don't let the enemy's plot to keep you eternally separated from God keep you quiet. Surely, you have something you can give God praise about. Even in my unbelief, God was faithful. He provided, protected, and pursued me. He "so loved the world that He gave His one and only Son, that whoever believes in Him shall not perish but have eternal life" (John 3:16, NIV). You don't need a pulpit or a platform to start. Be the light in your circle of influence.

REFLECT

1. How have you stewarded the pain in your life? Do you see it as entrustment or a burden?

2. What fear(s) have kept you from sharing your testimony with others?

Sustaining Grace

One of the greatest men in the New Testament is the Apostle Paul. Here is a man who is brilliant academically and high in status socially. He is known for persecuting Christians. The Lord radically transforms his life and Paul is now responsible for writing many books in the New Testament. In 2 Corinthians 12 verses 1 through 10, Paul speaks of the vision he had and by verse 9, we see Paul is pleading with Lord. Paul states in verse 8, "So to keep me from becoming conceited because of the surpassing greatness of the revelations, a thorn was given me in the flesh, a messenger of Satan to harass me, to keep me from becoming conceited" (ESV). We see here that the thorn is given to him to keep him humble. There are no biblical proofs as to exactly what this thorn is, but scholars have made some inferences. Some say it was a physical disease, or Jewish teachers contradicting his teaching. While others imply that it could be a spiritual weakness. Because Scripture was written through inspiration of the Holy Spirit, I believe God purposely did not tell us what the thorn was so that we can fill in the blank with our own aching thorn. Paul pleads with God to remove the thorn and God replies by saying, "My grace is sufficient for you, for my power is made perfect in weakness" (ESV).

I more than likely would have taken a step back and repeated myself in case God did not hear me. Three times he pleads, and God's answer is grace. By this point Paul is already doing ministry and leaving a legacy for Christ. Surely, God should heal him. Surely, he has access to God and should receive a divine manifestation. Instead, God tells him to rely on His grace. Why*? Because your weakness is God's open door for God's grace to work in your life*. Dealing with the difficulties of life should not deter us from the road of grace, but rather push us towards it.

We often define grace as unmerited favor. However, the Bible teaches us that grace is multifaceted (1 Peter 4:10) and has many functions. Grace saves us. Grace teaches us, and grace is an enabling force. As believers, we are saved by grace, but we are also sustained by grace. Titus 2 verse 11 through 12 reads, "For the grace of God that brings salvation has appeared to all men, teaching us that, denying ungodliness and worldly lusts, we should live soberly, righteously, and godly in the present age" (NKJV). Not only does grace enable our salvation, but it also sustains us to live according to God's standards in the present age. This can only be accessed by faith (Romans 5:1–2, NKJV) through prayer. Sometimes we can fall prey into believing everything must fall on the side of grace. But there must be a healthy tension between grace and works. We can't sit back and not participate in our time of pain because we are relying on grace. But we can rely on grace to do the work needed to grow, heal and maintain a state of homeostasis. As my husband once said, "If you are not growing in grace, then you are growing in works. And if you are growing by works, then you are really struggling because you are doing things in your own strength and not God's" (Dr. Tito Tirado).

There were many times I wanted to seek revenge against people who wronged me. I got tired of being mistreated, especially after I believed I was physically free. But God's grace sustained me as I purposed to learn about Him. I want to encourage you to "grow in the grace and knowledge of our Lord and Savior Jesus Christ" (2 Peter 2:18, NKJV). His power is made perfect in your weakness. In Isaiah 43:7 God declares these words, "Everyone who is called by My name, Whom I have created for My glory; I have formed him, yes, I have made him" (NJKV). You were created to know Him, love Him, and live with Him for His glory. He is your potter, and you are His clay. You are the branch, and He is the vine. Stay connected to Him and His grace shall be sufficient for you.

REFLECTION

1. When you hear the word grace, what comes to mind?

___

___

___

2. Sometimes the answers to our prayers are yes, no or wait. What no's have you received from God that you now see as blessings in disguise?

___

___

___

3. When was the last time you prayed and asked God to make His grace sufficient for you?

___

___

___

Everlasting Life

Jesus Christ died so I that I could win. He was wounded for my transgressions, yet by His stripes I am healed. I would love to say that the life I will live long after the writing on these pages shall be painless. Unfortunately, that's untrue. All I have to do is turn on the news at any given moment and the radio is appalling. For every 10 negative headlines, there is often not a positive one. The violence, wars, sickness, poverty, injustice, and climate devastation in our world are a constant reality of the fallen world we live in. That's not surprising because the Bible tells us in John 16:33, "In the world you will have trouble; but be of good cheer, I have overcome the world" (NKJV). Jesus spends time in John 16 discussing with His disciples His departure and what is to come. As a student of Christ, I know He never spoke without purpose.

One of the aspects of teaching that was stressed to us in our professional developments is the learning target. Administrators would observe classrooms and expect a display of the learning target around the classroom. Essentially, the learning target is a means to communicate with students what should be mastered by the end of class and through which evidence they will know they have mastered the specific skill. Jesus as the greatest teacher of all knew about learning targets before someone in education came to coin the phrase. The beginning of John 16:33 starts off with, "These things I have spoken unto you, that in Me, ye might have peace" (KJV). Though in this world we experience tribulations, Jesus's learning target for His disciples and the world was simple; in ME ye might have peace. The Greek word for ye might have is ἔχω echō. The phrase is written in the present tense, in an active voice and subjunctive mood. The subjunctive mood is the verb form used to express a wish, a suggestion, a command, or a condition that is contrary to fact. Therefore, it is obvious that not only was Jesus' uttering words that would impact the lives of His disciples then, but His words would echo in the hearts of the generations to come. In addition, He understood that peace in a world filled with tribulations is contradictory. But He doesn't leave us hanging and provides Himself as the source of peace.

In her last days of battling cancer, my husband asked his former wife a prevalent question, "Are you mad with God?" To his biggest surprise she answered, "Why would I be mad at God? If He heals me, I win. If He doesn't heal me, I win." Oh, what manner of faith! You see, Traci Tirado understood that Christ died on the cross for the forgiveness of her sins and that in Him, she had eternal life. She understood this well enough to die in peace, not angry at God or the world for the wound cancer had caused or any other wound she had ever experienced. Why? Because Jesus Christ was wounded so that she could win. Though Traci's story is not exactly like mine or yours, nor is my story exactly like yours, one thing I know for sure is, receiving salvation by faith through Jesus Christ has given me peace beyond understanding. So, until the day I meet my Savior and all those whom I love who have chosen eternity with Christ, I am convinced that being a partaker in Christ's sufferings, through my own tribulations, has wounded me, not so I can lose. But I have been wounded to win. It is my prayer that finishing this book does not truly mean the end. I may never get to meet you in this lifetime, but I want to spend eternity with you. Roman 10:9 says, "that if you CONFESS with your mouth the Lord Jesus and BELIEVE in your heart that God has raised Him from the dead, you will be SAVED" (NKJV). If you have already done this, I can't wait to spend forever with you in heaven. Please know that your labor is not in vain. Stay the course, run the race with endurance, "For in Him we live, and move, and have our being" (Acts 17:28, NKJV).

But if you haven't, it is my utmost desire that today will be different than yesterday. That today, though we may have never met, by faith, I am holding your hands as you choose to pray this prayer with me.

"God, I recognize that I have not lived my life for You up until now. I have been living for myself and that is wrong. I need You in my life; I want You in my life. I acknowledge the completed work of Your Son Jesus Christ in giving His life for me on the cross at Calvary, and I long to receive the forgiveness you have made freely available to me through this sacrifice. Come into my life now, Lord. Take up residence in my heart and be my king, my Lord, and my Savior. From this day forward, I will no longer be controlled by sin, or the desire to please myself, but I will follow You all the days of my

life. Those days are in Your hands. I ask this in Jesus' precious and holy name. Amen."

If you decided to repent of your sins and receive Christ today, welcome to God's family. I urge you to tell someone about your new faith in Christ and to seek fellowship with other followers of Jesus. I know you have many questions and will need support. The way forward is not done alone. So, start praying, reading God's Word, and actively searching for a Bible believing church where you can worship your risen king, Jesus Christ, and grow in His likeness. Though the journey may seem scary, please know that you are not alone. I am praying for you and can't wait to meet you. If not in this lifetime, we will surely meet in the next. For it is then and only then our Heavenly Father shall present us the winning trophy engraved with these words:

> "Well done, good and faithful servant" (Matthew 25:21, NKJV).

AFTERWORDS

Dear Reader,

I am a woman walking whole because I can have the memories without the pain while creating new stories despite the pain. In 2008 I told my college roommates that I wanted to write a book. It took ten years to give birth to this baby. Writing this book was probably one of the hardest things I have ever done. I did not realize how much emotional pull having to relive many painful memories would have on me. I wrote keeping in mind that my goal is not for anyone who has done me wrong to be exposed. I wanted to be authentic to the events of my past, my emotions, and their outcome. In the beginning, I would be mad at myself because it took me this long to write the book. Nonetheless, I am seeing that God's timing has been best. Had I written this book any time before now, I would have bled through these pages with bitterness, anger, unforgiveness and most of all revenge. All these would not have brought glory to God or ministered to anyone.

My trials and tribulations are the cries of many others, but this is my testimony. I lived through them. I survived them and God has given me an opportunity to share that journey with you. I pray that if nothing else, this book has shown you that things could be worse, but things could also be better. Whether you find yourself amid pain or on the side of healing, may you always know that there is purpose in your pain. Getting divine help, counseling or the support of your community is not a sign of weakness, but strength. God never wastes a hurt if you choose to entrust Him with your wounds. He is not the author of confusion or evil, but He can weave our wounds into the design and purpose of your life.

Until next time, I am rooting for you.

Njiba Tirado

www.njibatirado.com

ACKNOWLEDGEMENTS

It is by the grace of God, His strength, and the power of the Holy Spirit that I have been able to complete this book. However, I would be remiss to not acknowledge and thank the many individuals God placed on my path to make this a reality.

My husband, Dr. Tito Tirado: Thank you for taking a leap of faith with me. You love me like Christ loves His Church and I couldn't have done this without you. I can't wait to create lifelong memories with you. You allowed me to sacrifice time with you and our kids, so that I could finish this project. You encouraged me to write the book. You prayed for me and with me. Thank you for being selfless and showing me what abiding in unconditional love means. I love you.

My children, Samantha, Christian, Tito & Kaleb: It's an honor to call you mine. I pray the Lord gives me many years to see all that He wishes to accomplish in your lives. Thank you for sacrificing bonding time so I could complete this project.

My siblings, Suzanne, Naomi, Nathan & Anna: I eagerly wait for the day we will all be reunited again. If God asked me who I wanted as siblings, I would be honored to choose each one of you. Thank you for being part of my story.

The Tshieks, Beyas & Kumuambas: Thank you for picking up where David & Nadine Kasonga could not finish the job. I can't tell my story without you all being a part of it.

LaShondra & Edwin Rice: God knew what He was doing when He placed you both on my path. I still can't believe I get to be your daughter. Thank you for loving me as such.

My Samaritan, Kedra Renee: I am beyond grateful for our friendship. I would never die for you because Christ did that already, but I'll take a bullet with a vest on. Love you friend.

My team, Marvin Manigault Jr., Ladawn Hodges, Tracey Liverman, Tiffany White & Anna Segre: Thank you for helping me make this project a reality.

Dr. Stan & Connie Mitchel: Earning a bachelor's and master's would have never been possible without you. I pray one day I can be as much of a blessing to someone as you were to me.

My professional mentors, Bobby Surry, Joseph Edwards, Greg Henderson & Corey Gordon: Thank you for always believing in me and pushing me to my fullest potential.

My friend, Leia Hardimon: Most people say let's do something and never follow up. Thank you for doing life with me. I am grateful Traci picked you as a best friend and godmother to our son Christian.

My catalyst, Allison Moore: Thank you for igniting the spark in me to write this book at the FEARLESS Conference and assisting me through our writing group.

My ESOL teacher, Mrs. Guthmiller: I am the proficient English speaker that I am because of your diligence to education. Thank you for helping me grow.

My college adviser, Dr. Michael Meyer: Thank you for imparting wisdom to me that would help me change the trajectory of my life.

My freshman roomies, Natalie & Tara: Ten years later, I choose to believe being random roommates was divinely orchestrated. Thank you for being my friends.

My CNU International Crew: There are too many people to name, but when I felt alone on that campus, you all gave me a place to belong. Thank you.

My youth leader, Lindsay Conrad: Thank you for keeping your heart running after Christ, enough so that your love for Him would keep me in the faith during the hardest times of my life.

These institutions: Regent University, Christopher Newport University, Menchville High School, Dozier Middle School & Mamu Lumingu for the education they provided me with.

The following churches: Hidenwood Presbyterian, Calvary Chapel Newport News & Coastal Community Church for shaping and molding me through my sanctification process.

My CORE sister Sonya: Thank you for being a part of my restoration journey. Our friendship is a reminder of how God's ways are better than ours.

Tiphani Montgomery: Thank you for using your platform to help others grow, not only business wise, but also spiritually.

My friend Tati Council: Thank you for keeping me accountable in writing this book and always checking on my progress. I appreciate you.

Marshawn Evans: Thank you for helping me Believe Bigger.

David Seamands: Thank you for helping me heal my damaged emotions.

My friends, family & supporters: Thank you for doing life with me.

To those I have wounded: I pray you find it in your heart to forgive me.

To those who have wounded me: Thank you for being part of my character formation.

Made in the USA
Middletown, DE
08 November 2022